TEN STORIES TO DEVELOP A LEGAL MIND

COLLECTION OF SHORT ESSAYS & ARTICLES

2015
LEUVEN, BELGIUM
RAMIN LEV

Published independently

© Ramin Lev (Aliyev)   *TEN STORIES TO DEVELOP A LEGAL MIND*

The majority of the papers collected in this book, excluding its Chapter 2, were written by the author in 2014-2015 in LEUVEN, Belgium. This is the first edition of the book.

The book can be a good source of information for analytical thinking. Its target audience may include students, professors, scholar, lawyers, judges, prosecutors, policymakers etc.

Mr. Ramin Lev (Aliyev) is a 40 years old lawyer born in the Lev village of Kelbadjar district on 27 April 1978 when Azerbaijan Republic was still a part of the former Soviet Union. He represents a generation, which suffered the detrimental consequences of an unjust war. Ramin Lev holds a Master Degree in Law (Baku State University, Azerbaijan Republic) and another Master Degree in Law, Society and Religion (KU Leuven, Belgium). He has specialised in the sphere of legal expertise and information analysis. His expertise lies in following areas:- legal counselling; legal teaching; (Public Law, Fundamentals of Law, Constitutional Law, Economic Analysis of Law, Law, Religion and Society, Criminal Law, Public International Law, International Human Rights Law, Law of the Cultural Heritage etc.); and information analysis.

Email: raminlev@gmail.com

Telephone: + 99 455 318 31 05

Contents

FOREWORD — 3

CHAPTER 1. ESSAYS — 5

ESSAY NO 1. THE RIGHT TO LIFE V. THE "RIGHT TO DIE": COMPARATIVE ANALYSIS OF THE DIANE PRETTY CASE — 6

INTRODUCTION — 6

A COUPLE OF WORDS ABOUT THE RIGHT TO LIFE AND THE RIGHT TO DIE — 6

BRIEF SUMMARY OF THE PRETTY CASE — 8

MRS PRETTY'S 'RIGHT TO DIE' BEFORE ECHR — 9

'RIGHT TO DIE' IN DOMESTIC HUMAN RIGHTS LAW (DHRL) AND INTERNATIONAL HUMAN RIGHTS LAW (IHRL) — 10

CANON LAW: IS THERE ANY ROOM FOR THE 'RIGHT TO DIE? — 12

CONCLUSIONS — 13

BIBLIOGRAPHY — 16

ESSAY NO 2. APOSTOLIC LETTER "MOTU PROPRIO" OMNIUM IN MENTEM OF THE SUPREME PONTIFF BENEDICT XVI ON SEVERAL AMENDMENTS TO THE CODE OF CANON LAW — 18

INTRODUCTION — 18

GENERAL REMARKS ON NORM-CREATION/REVISION: SECULAR LEGAL SYSTEMS AND CANON LAW — 19

THE SPECIAL STATUS OF THE CHURCH IN LAW CREATION — 21

THE FIRST AMENDMENT – THE DIACONATE IN THE HOLY ORDER — 21

THE SECOND AMENDMENT – SUBORDINATE CLAUSE "AND HAS NOT LEFT IT BY A FORMAL ACT" — 23

CONCLUSIONS   *24*

BIBLIOGRAPHY   *26*

ESSAY NO 3. 'THE CANONICAL DOCTRINE OF RECEPTION' BY JAMES CORIDEN   *28*

INTRODUCTION   *28*

II. ANY NEW RULE HAS TO BE ACCEPTED BY THE COMMUNITY IN ORDER TO BECOME AN EFFECTIVE GUIDE!   *29*

III. PERSPECTIVES OF THE DOCTRINE OF RECEPTION IN MODERN AGES   *32*

BIBLIOGRAPHY   *36*

ESSAY NO 4. CASE OF ISLAM-ITTIHAD ASSOCIATION V. AZERBAIJAN REPUBLIC   *37*

INTRODUCTION   *37*

DETAILS OF THE CASE: AGENDA AND ACTIVITIES OF THE ASSOCIATION, DOMESTIC LEGISLATION AND THE COURT FINDINGS   *38*

STRIKING BALANCE BETWEEN THE NATIONAL INTERESTS AND UNIVERSAL VALUES: A LEGAL NECESSITY OR A LEGAL CIRCUMVENTION   *40*

FACTORS AFFECTING FORB ENVIRONMENTS IN AZERBAIJAN POSITIVELY AND NEGATIVELY   *42*

PUBLIC AND PRIVATE ASPECTS OF FORB   *43*

CONCLUSIONS   *44*

BIBLIOGRAPHY   *46*

CHAPTER 2. ARTICLES   *49*

ARTICLE NO 1. FREEDOM OF RELIGION AND BELIEF IN AZERBAIJAN (FORB): CURRENT LEGAL REGIME, CONTEMPORARY CHALLENGES AND SAFEGUARDS   *50*

INTRODUCTİON   *50*

I. THE LEGAL FORB REGİME İN AZERBAİJAN REPUBLİC	51
II. INSTITUTIONAL SAFEGUARDS FOR FORB IN AZERBAIJAN	57
III. CHALLENGES FOR FORB	58
CONCLUSIONS	59
USED LITERATURE	62
ARTICLE NO 2. APOCALYPSES ALREADY KNOCK AT OUR DOORS: TWO 'INVISIBLE' CHANCES FOR SURVIVING...	64
INTRODUCTION	64
PAYING THE PRICE: 'CRYING' FIGURES	65
FUELLING CONFLICT: IS THE UN SECURITY SYSTEM EFFECTIVE ENOUGH TO PREVENT?	70
CONCLUSIONS	77
BIBLIOGRAPHY	83
CHAPTER 3. OPINION	85
HOW REVENGE LESSENS THE IMPORTANCE OF REPORTING IN CONFLICT RESOLUTION	86
THE EURASIAN ECONOMIC UNION: PERSPECTIVES AND RISKS	88
WHEN HISTORY REPEATS ITSELF...	92
MY EXPERIENCES AS AN EX-TEAM MEMBER: SECRETS OF EFFECTIVE TEAMS	98
ENCOURAGEMENT HERITAGE	101

Foreword

Dear reader!

From the very beginning, I would like to make you aware of the fact that this book is not going to tell you which methods and ways are necessary for a human being to develop a legal mind. On the contrary, it will narrate 10 various short stories related to the central problems of modernity including, euthanasia, armed conflicts, geopolitical confrontations, radicalism and separatism, international cooperation, the problem of effectiveness of legal regulation etc. After familiarizing yourselves with the facts and legal norms to be applied to each case, hopefully, you will be able to judge righteously and legally. In other words, the book intends to change your way of perceiving various threats of our times and legal approaches used to deal with those threats in an effective, timely and operative manner.

I also hope that the book will meet, at least, some of your concerns regarding the role and importance of law within our society. I find it very fit-for-purpose because of the following reason. Contemporary societies are divided into two opposing fronts while trying to formulate their attitude towards law. The first group views law as a set of rights and freedoms. Thus, law for them is a very useful concept. The second group is of the opinion that law consists of numerous restrictions imposed on their rights and freedoms. Of course, we can notice a minority group of intellectuals who are capable to find the desirable middle between the above-mentioned two extremes. In my humble opinion, real life situations and circumstances are extremely complex and difficult to accept law as rights and freedoms, restrictions and prohibitions, or a combination of both.

This book is an attempt to address that hidden aspect of law. Strict, red borderlines are not applicable to the legal space. We should never try to define the content and essence of law by drawing lines, by dividing, or by combining it. Yes, it is true that sometimes law can be a right, a privilege. The subject of law can earn something thanks to that right. Nevertheless, one should not forget that each right gives birth to a subsequent obligation (e.g., right to life equals obligation not to try to kill others). From that point of view, law should be perceived as a single and whole, indivisible, divine being designed to help us to complete our mission on the Earth. For that purpose, we have to study law, consisting of various blocks (Spirit of law, enormous official texts, authoritative will, customs etc.), as much and in depth as we can. We shouldn't study law in order to be sure that it exists. Because, like the truth, law is always out there. On the contrary, we should study law only if we have no single doubt regarding its existence. As Mevlana says, "You task is not to seek for love, but merely to seek and find all the barriers within yourself that you have built against it".

Please, note that the text of the book has not been edited by a native speaker. Therefore, I find it appropriate to deliver my apologies to the reader for any kind of mistakes or omissions, or technical inconsistencies. I would also like to express my deepest thanks to all who bought this book. You time, money and energy spent on it is sincerely appreciated. I wish you an enjoyable reading.

Finally, I must admit that I have been so blessed throughout my school and university years to have had excellent teachers, professors and lecturers. Thank you so much, holy human beings! I do always remember and value you!

Chapter 1. Essays

ESSAY NO 1. THE RIGHT TO LIFE V. THE "RIGHT TO DIE": COMPARATIVE ANALYSIS OF THE DIANE PRETTY CASE

Keywords: Right to life; "right to die"; "euthanasia debate", "Pretty case; Canon Law; Secular Law.

Introduction

Are human beings free in disposing of their lives? It is a difficult question to answer. "We are stewards, but not owners, of the life God has entrusted in us. It is not ours to dispose of"[1]. This is a very strict religious prohibition against the right to die. It is based upon the following religious principles: God alone is the creator of everything including human life; Human life is sacred to God.

Nowadays, the problem has already become more than a religious one. It is a complex issue. This essay tries to find an appropriate answer to the question whether the prohibition of the right to die is absolute or relative under current circumstances. It is a minor effort to formulate a compromised attitude with regard to the problem.

The Judgement of the Pretty Case[2] constitutes the principal foundation of the analysis in the essay due to the important role of this case in transferring all "right to die debates" from philosophical, moral and religious sphere to the legal domain. The analysis have been put into various sections under the fitting titles, each of which is related to a separate subject-matter.

A couple of words about the right to life and the right to die

The right to life has only positive perspectives and may be explained as a legal opportunity to become into existence and survive in the womb[3], be born,

---

[1] Catechism of the Catholic Church, paragraph 2280: http://www.vatican.va/archive/ENG0015/__P7Z.HTM
[2] Pretty v. United Kingdom, ECHR Judgement of 20 April 2002.
[3] "L'Odyssée de la Vie" by "CVP Grupo Educacional": https://www.youtube.com/watch?v=uj29OOAGc38

grow up and live in dignity till the possibly maximum age. And the dignity of a person must be recognized in every human being from conception to natural death[1]. In biological sciences, chronological 'life cycles' are distinguished. For example, Dr Thomas Armstrong defines twelve stages of human life: pre-birth (potential), birth (hope), infancy (ages 0-3), early childhood (ages 3-6), middle childhood (ages 6-8), late childhood (ages 9-11), adolescence (ages 12-20), early adulthood (ages 20-35), midlife (ages 35-50), mature adulthood (ages 50-80) and death and dying[2]. Legally, rights arising within each life circle are different in essence and form.

Historical sources prove the fact that, the right to die (euthanasia and suicide) were completely legalized and widespread in classical antiquity[3]. However after the emergence of Judaism and Christianity, ideas like sanctity of life, sovereignty of God on human life etc. gained strong moral force. The mentioned ideas, originating from the so-called divine law, reflected in all appropriate scriptures of the Judaism[4], Christianity[5], and starting from the VII century Islam[6] were gradually transformed into the positive law in the course of centuries.

Thus, the concept of *the 'right to die' can be taken into consideration as a negative or opposite side of the right to life*. We have to mention more public equivalent of the right to die – *euthanasia* which is a medical term and originates

---

[1] Instruction Dignitas Personae on Certain Bioethical Questions, 2008, paragraph 1
[2] Thomas Armstrong, The Human Odyssey: Navigating the twelve Stages of Life. New York: Sterling, 2008.
[3] Ian Dowbiggin. A Concise History of Euthanasia: Life, Death, God and Medicine (Critical Issues in History). Lanham Md., Rowmann and Littlefield, 2005: http://ahr.oxfordjournals.org/content/111/3/807.full.pdf+html).
[4] I Samuel 31:1-6, II Samuel 1:5-10, Talmudic sources, Semahot 1:1, Avodah Zara 18a. For the reprinted electronic text of the article by Dr Fred Rosner titled 'Euthanasia: Jewish Biblical and Rabbinic Sources' see: http://www.myjewishlearning.com/beliefs/Issues/Bioethics/Euthanasia/Biblical_and_Rabbinic.shtml?p=1.
[5] Genesis 1:27, Deuteronomy 30:19, Job 10:8-12, Job 31:15, Psalm 51:5, Psalm 95:6, Psalm 100:3, Psalm 119:73, Psalm 138:8, Psalm 139:13-16, Isaiah 44:2 etc.
[6] Quran verses 29 (Chapter 4), 151 (Chapter 6), 66 (Chapter 22) etc. 'The sanctity of human life is a basic concept in Islam' by Dr A. Majid Katme: https://www.spuc.org.uk/about/muslim-division/euthanasia

from the Greek language (eu, "well", and thanatos, "death")[1]. The word "euthanasia" is usually understood as the taking of an adult life, thus differing from other similar notions like suicide, infanticide, and genocide[2].

In practice, "active euthanasia" (producing death) and "passive euthanasia" (withdrawal of any kind of life-supporting interventions) are distinguished. Also, euthanasia may be voluntary (patient requests to end his/her life) and involuntary (euthanasia is requested by a third person)[3]. The concept of paternalism is an opposite of euthanasia, as 'the interference of a state or an individual with another person, against their will, and defended or motivated by a claim that the person interfered with will be better off or protected from harm'[4].

Besides the religious, theoretical and doctrinal attitude towards euthanasia as presented above, let's mention several important court practices on this issue. So, the influential domestic "right to die cases" are Karen Ann Quinlan Case[5] (USA), Nancy Cruzan Case[6] (USA), Terry Schiavo Case[7] (USA), Chantal Sebire Case[8] (France), Eluana Englaro Case[9] (Italy) etc. What about the Pretty case, it is one of the first "right to die" cases seen by the European Court of Human Rights (ECHR).

Brief summary of the Pretty Case

Mrs Diane Pretty (1958-2002) was a British national. She challenged the dominant stereotypes in the minds of people by trying to change the paternalist policies of the state, and the 'hybrid' (religious, moral and legal) principle which

---

[1] 'Euthanasia is an act of painless killing of a patient suffering from an incurable and painful disease or in an irreversible coma': http://www.oxforddictionaries.com/definition/english/euthanasia
[2] See: http://www.thefreedictionary.com
[3] Christian BYK, 'L'euthanasie en droit français», Revue internationale de droit comparé'. Vol. 58 N°2,2006
[4] Stanford Encyclopaedia of Philosophy: http://plato.stanford.edu/entries/paternalism/
[5] http://en.wikipedia.org/wiki/Karen_Ann_Quinlan
[6] http://en.wikipedia.org/wiki/Cruzan_v._Director,_Missouri_Department_of_Health
[7] http://en.wikipedia.org/wiki/Terri_Schiavo_case
[8] http://fr.wikipedia.org/wiki/Affaire_Chantal_S%C3%A9bire
[9] http://en.wikipedia.org/wiki/Eluana_Englaro

absolutely eliminates the possibility of choosing the time and form of death by the human being.

Several years before her death she had been diagnosed with a disease known as MND[1]. The most terrible nature of this illness is that over time patients become completely paralysed. However their mind remains as sharp as ever.

Therefore Mrs Pretty was trying to urge all to help her to die. Suicide Act of 1961[2], Article 1 states that 'The rule of law whereby it is a crime for a person to commit suicide is hereby abrogated'. Nevertheless, its Article 2 maintains criminal liability for complicity in another's suicide. Because of this legal impediment, nobody could help her to commit suicide.

She asked the British Director of the Public Prosecutions to issue an undertaking that a person helping her to commit suicide would not be held responsible for killing her. But the authorities of the UK refused to do that. She took the case to ECHR after failing at domestic courts.

Mrs Pretty's 'right to die' before ECHR

The Applicant's lawyers based their position on several arguments (Mrs Pretty had terminal illness, her sufferings were intolerable etc.) and articles 2 (right to life), 3 (Prohibition of Torture), 8 (Right to Respect for Private and Family Life), 9 (Freedom of Thought, Conscience and Religion), 14 (Prohibition of Discrimination) of the Convention.

In my humble opinion, the alleged violations of Articles 8, 9 and 14, like the alleged breach of Article 3, might be considered as the "secondary violations" by

---

[1] Motor neurone disease: http://www.nhs.uk/conditions/Motor-neurone-disease/Pages/Introduction.aspx
[2] http://www.legislation.gov.uk/ukpga/Eliz2/9-10/60

the applicant. Probably, she considered the violation of Article 2 as the major violation. It becomes obvious from her claims in which she thought Article 2 contained the right to die as well.

The Court found no violations. But the Court 'satisfied' the Applicant by only expressing its sympathy to her for the reason that she apprehended the inescapability of the prospect of "a distressing death" in case she would had been left without the possibility of putting an end to her life[1]. ECHR also rejected to recognize the claims that 'Article 2 of the Convention provided a right to die'[2].

She told on this occasion: "The Law has taken all my rights away"[3]. In the event, the patient died on 11 May 2002, at the age of 43 without any interventions. Immediately after Mrs Diane Pretty's death, her husband Mr Brian Pretty told 'the manner of her death was the one thing she had foreseen and was afraid of'[4].

'Right to die' in Domestic Human Rights Law (DHRL) and International Human Rights Law (IHRL)

The dilemma of euthanasia is a multidimensional issue with moral, ethical, religious, economic etc. perceptions. Apparently, this complexity has caused a confrontation within the modern societies. The world is divided into two opposite fronts with regards to euthanasia. Consequently, the domestic legal systems have to reflect this controversy.

On the other hand, a great majority of the secular, domestic legal systems still exclude any forms of euthanasia. As distinguished Judge Christian Byk emphasises, "And yet human rights law seems loftily to ignore exercise of individual

---

[1] Pretty v. United Kingdom, Judgement of 20 April 2002, paragraph 55.
[2] Pretty v. United Kingdom, Judgement of 20 April 2002, paragraph 40.
[3] http://www.theguardian.com/society/2002/apr/29/health.medicineandhealth
[4] http://news.bbc.co.uk/2/hi/health/1983941.stm

autonomy with respect to death"[1]. For instance, The British legal system totally excluded the 'right to die' in the Pretty Case.

On the other hand, there is an emerging 'minority' of national legal systems in Europe which have already started supporting the 'right to die'. According to R.Cohen-Almagor, "The legislation lays out the terms for doctors to end the lives of patients who are hopelessly ill and are suffering unbearably"[2]. Under the Belgian Act of Euthanasia (2002), Article 2, "Euthanasia is defined as intentionally terminating life by someone other than the person concerned, at the latter's request"[3].

What about IHRL, it apparently does not contain any provisions implying the 'right to die'. However this may be expected to happen soon due to several factors. *First of all*, the similarity of the ideas initiating the 'right to die' with the ideas giving rise to human rights may lead to such crisscrossing. In the Pretty Case the applicant built the main structure of her claim on *the principles of morality and human dignity*. Likewise, Antal Szerletics points out that "Mrs Pretty submitted that the suffering which she faced qualifies as *degrading treatment and violates human dignity*"[4]. And the authoritative IHRL doctrine is of the opinion that "Although the binding force of the human rights obligations must rest ultimately in treaty or custom, *the inspiration for these obligations lies in 'morality', 'justice', 'ethics' or a simple regard for the dignity of Mankind*"[5].

Secondly, the recognition of *the fourth generation of human rights* imposed by the interdependent relationships among science, economics, and politics and so on is already on the agenda of IHRL which may also include the 'right to die'.

---

[1] Euthanasia: Ethical and Human Aspect, Volume I. "Euthanasia and the right to life: Pretty Case" by Christian Byk, pp. 109. Strasbourg 2003.
[2] R. Cohen-Almagor, Belgian Euthanasia Law : a critical analysis, J Med Ethics 2009;35:436–439, page 436
[3] Ethical Perspectives 9 (2002), 2-3, p.182
[4] Antal Szerletics. Paternalism and Euthanasia: The Case of Diane Pretty before the European Court of Human Rights, published at 'Diritto e questioni pubbliche', p. 480 Palermo, 2011 (available at: http://www.dirittoequestionipubbliche.org/page/2010_n10/3-11_studi_A_Szerletics.pdf
[5] Textbook on International Law, by Martin Dixon, 7th Edition, 2013, p.354.

For instance, Fernando Falcón y Tella includes in the list of these new categories "*the great developments in the area of biotechnology or the Internet*"[1].

Canon Law: is there any room for the 'right to die?

The Pope Francis has recently condemned the right to die movement and denounced euthanasia as '*sin against God*'[2]. And the official position of the Holy See has also been well reflected in Canon Law which is "… a system of a religious law ultimately based upon a thick natural law theory as well as claims rooted in revealed truth"[3].

Canon Law has historically developed the concept of 'miserabiles personae', in order to possibly maximum extent, to mitigate the situation of those and to protect them all who, due to their aggravated life conditions, may be willing to suspect the inviolability of the right to life principle. All terminally-ill patients "suffering from debilitating, long-term diseases"[4] fall under that category. Also, St Thomas Aquinas sets forth a very authoritative argument which lays down that "*The power of jurisdiction is not granted a man for his own benefit, but for the good of the people and for the glory of God*"[5].

The superiority of pro-life provisions against euthanasia has repeatedly been expressed in modern ages from many perspectives. For instance, Lumen Gentium (1964) outlines "*the holiness of life to each*" and reminds all "*they are united with the suffering Christ in a special way for the salvation of the world*"[6]. John J.

---

[1] Fernando Falcón y Tella, Challenges for Human Rights, by Koninklijke Brill NV, Leiden, the Netherlands, 2007, p. 66
[2] http://www.telegraph.co.uk/news/worldnews/the-pope/11233347/Pope-Francis-denounces-euthanasia-as-sin-against-God.html
[3] John J. Coughlin, Canon Law: A Comparative Study with Anglo-American Legal Theory, Oxford 2011, and p.140
[4] "The Spirit of Classical Canon Law" by R.H.Helmholz, p. 128. University of Georgia Press, 1996.
[5] St Thomas Aquinas, Summa Theologia, Volume V, Part III, Second Section and Supplement Q. 8, Art. 5, 2007 edition, New York, p.2586.
[6] Dogmatic Constitution on the Church Lumen Gentiium, Chapter V – 40, 41, 1964

Coughlin reminds Cardinal Ratzinger's 'Statement of Six Principles' (2004), second and third ones of which consider abortion and euthanasia as having a greater moral weight than other human life taking issues[1].

Evangelium Vitae (1995) stresses *'the incomparable worth of human person'*, includes euthanasia in the list of new threats to human life, and re-confirms that all those threats are *'a supreme dishonour to the Creator'*. It is not a secret that human rights have already found the solemn affirmation in the world but are still being largely denied in practice. The reason for such a denial *"lies in a notion of freedom which exalts the isolated individual in and absolute way, and gives no place to solidarity, to openness to others and service of them"*[2]. Also, willing to prevent the unpredictable catastrophic consequences of the uncontrolled scientific researches, Donum Vitae (1987) outlines the necessity of the intervention of secular law and institutions[3].

In my humble opinion, the major point is also to be able to find 'the gold middle' between the realisation of the opportunities created by human freedom and limitations on that freedom for the sake of *'salus annimarum'*[4] and *common good*. Canon 227 of the Code of Canon Law, for example, stipulates that *"The lay Christian faithful, while using the recognized freedom, are to take care that their actions are imbued with the spirit of Gospel"*[5].

Conclusions

Nowadays human intellect is striving to save or prolong lives by the invention and use of new medicines and technologies. Unfortunately, it is not always possible and probably will never become 'a luxury of human beings'. May be this

---

[1] John J. Coughlin, Canon Law: A Comparative Study with Anglo-American Legal Theory, Oxford 2011, and p.147
[2] Evangelium Vitae on the Value and Inviolability of Human Life of 1995, paragraph 19
[3] Encyclical Donum Vitae Instruction on respect for human life in its origin and on the dignity of procreation: replies to certain questions of the day, **22 February 1987**
[4] Salus Animarum Suprema Lex – Supreme Law is the Salvation of Souls
[5] Code of Canon Law, Latin-English Edition, 2012 second printing, p.67.

reality increases the ongoing tensions within our modern societies with regards to the possibility of deviations from the right to life.

Mrs Pretty's legal fight, both at the domestic and European levels, constituted one of the most typical court proceedings affected by the previously described confrontations. I will further try to formulate several questions in order to be able to evaluate the Pretty case from the challenging point of view. *Firstly*, was the admission of the contemporary medicine enough to establish legal foundations to give birth to the 'right to die'? *Secondly*, why were criterions such as 'immorality of the treatment', 'human dignity' and 'inadmissibility of human suffering' not sufficient for the Courts to recognise the 'right to die'? *Thirdly*, why did the law allow 'independent suicide', but forbid its assisted form?[1] *Fourthly*, why are other "licenced killings"[2] recognised and allowed. *Fifthly*, why were other arguments including caregivers' burden, right to refuse medical care etc. not taken on board?[3]

The most fit-for-purpose answers are to be found in Canon Law (discussed in an earlier section). But still the situation is very sensitive. If the secularised parts of the societies in the 'majority countries' gradually achieve concessions from their respective governments on this matter, what will happen then? Definitely, Article 2 of the Convention does not create any so-called 'right to die' as the right to life cannot involve its negative twin. But what if IHRL will somehow embody this 'right' in the future, as a very specific and rare kind of human 'right'?

In my humble opinion, this could be very detrimental to the human society as a whole. As already noted above, concepts like divine law, afterlife, salus animarum and so on could be effectively developed (in close cooperation and

---

[1] The problem is that patients or their family members and doctors apply to euthanasia illegally. For example, see the Chantal Sebire case (2008).
[2] Please see Article 2 of the Convention for the cases in which deprivation of life is allowed. In this context Article 15 (Derogation in time of Emergency) is also important.
[3] Euthanasia: right to life vs right to die, by Suresh Bada Math and Santosh K. Chaturvedi. Indian Journal of Medical Research, December 2012, 136 (6), pp. 899-902.

consultation with all appropriate sciences) into more target-oriented guidelines with the purpose of preventing the 'right to die' to become a comprehensively recognised tool of IHRL. The negotiation of a possible preventive international agreement might also be considered as an effective instrument. Furthermore, the inclusion of the motivative and prohibitive legal principles and norms in the Code of Canon Law seems also appropriate, as "…the Code is to be regarded as an indispensable instrument to ensure order both in individual and social life, and also in the Church's own activity"[1].

---

[1] Apostolic Constitution Sacrae Disciplinae Leges of 1983. See the Code of Canon Law, Latin-English Edition 2012, page xxx.

Bibliography

1. Catechism of the Catholic Church, paragraph 2280: http://www.vatican.va/archive/ENG0015/__P7Z.HTM
2. Textbook on International Law, by Martin Dixon, 7th Edition, 2013
3. Euthanasia: Ethical and Human Aspect, Volume I. "Euthanasia and the right to life: Pretty Case" by Christian Byk, pp. 109-131. Strasbourg 2003.
4. Thomas Armstrong, The Human Odyssey: Navigating the twelve Stages of Life. New York: Sterling, 2008
5. St Thomas Aquinas, Summa Theologia, Volume V, Part III, Second Section and Supplement, 2007 edition, New York
6. S. E. Wallace and A. Eser, 'Suicide and Euthanasia: The Rights of Personhood', 1981
7. R.H.Helmholz, 'The Spirit of Classical Canon Law' 1996.
8. Ian Dowbiggin, 'A Concise History of Euthanasia: Life, Death, God and Medicine' (Critical Issues in History). Lanham Md., Rowmann and Littlefield, 2005
9. 'Euthanasia: Jewish Biblical and Rabbinic Sources' was published at 'Biomedical Ethics and Jewish Law' by KTAV (reprinted electronic version)
10. Commentary on Genesis 9, The Jewish Study Bible, Oxford University Press, 2004, p.25, Talmud b B K 91b, b Sanhedrin 57b
11. Antal Szerletics, 'Paternalism and Euthanasia: The Case of Diane Pretty before the European Court of Human Rights', published at 'Diritto e questioni pubbliche', p. 480 Palermo, 2011.
12. 'Euthanasia: right to life vs right to die' by Suresh Bada Math and Santosh K. Chaturvedi. Indian Journal of Medical Research, December 2012, 136 (6), pp. 899-902.
13. Christian BYK, 'L'euthanasie en droit français», Revue internationale de droit comparé'. Vol. 58 N°2, 2006.
14. Fernando Falcón y Tella, 'Challenges for Human Rights', by Koninklijke Brill NV, Leiden, the Netherlands, 2007
15. R. Cohen-Almagor, 'Belgian Euthanasia Law: a critical analysis', J Med Ethics 2009;35:436–439.
16. John J. Coughlin, 'Canon Law: A Comparative Study with Anglo-American Legal Theory', Oxford 2011.

Domestic legislative Acts

1. Suicide Act 1961
2. Human Rights Act 1998
3. The Belgian Act on Euthanasia of (2002)

Canon Law documents

1. Pastoral Constitution on the Church in the Modern World Gaudium et Spes (1995)
2. Code of Canon Law (1983)
3. Apostolic Constitution Sacrae Disciplinae Leges (1983)
4. Dogmatic Constitution on the Church Lumen Gentiium (1964)
5. Encyclical Letter Evangelium Vitae on the Value and Inviolability of Human Life (1995)
6. Encyclical Donum Vitae Instruction on respect for human life in its origin and on the dignity of procreation: replies to certain questions of the day (1987)
7. Encyclical Dignitas Personae on Certain Bioethical Questions (2008)

Cases

1. Pretty v. United Kingdom, ECHR Judgement of (2002)
2. Karen Ann Quinlan Case, USA, New Jersey Supreme Court (1976)
3. Cruzan v. Director, Missouri Department of Health, USA Supreme Court (1990)
4. Terry Schiavo Case, , USA, the last Judgement by Florida Appeals Court (2005)
5. Chantal Sebire Case, France, Le tribunal de grande instance de Dijon (2008)
6. Eluana Englaro Case, Italy, Corte Suprema di Cassazione (2008)

Essay No 2. Apostolic Letter "Motu Proprio" Omnium in Mentem of the Supreme Pontiff Benedict XVI on Several Amendments to the Code of Canon Law

Keywords: Code of Canon Law; Apostolic Letter "Motu Proprio" Omnium in Mentem; amendments to the code of Canon Law.

Introduction

Apostolic Letter Motu Proprio Omnium in Mentem of the Supreme Pontiff Benedict XVI on Several Amendments to the Code of Canon Law ("Motu Proprio") is a very important ecclesiastical document promulgated on 26 October 2009 which amended several canons in the Code. The Canons under question (1008, 1009 and 1086 § 1, 1117, 1124) were studied for some time by the appropriate Church institutions in order to determine their necessity or suitability. The outcomes of the examinations were in favour of making necessary amendments to all five canons.

The document itself is structured like many other apostolic letters. Although there is no any structural division in the text of the instrument, I would like to divide it formally into the following sections. The introductory part of the canonical document quotes a passage from the Apostolic Constitution Sacrae Disciplinae Leges, apparently, to substantiate the possibility and necessity of amendments to the Code. It also outlines the importance of establishing a legal balance between the theological doctrine and canonical legislation and pastoral usefulness of the prescriptions.

The central part of the text has been dedicated to the explanation of the subject-matter of the document. § 3 discusses the amendment to canons on the sacrament of Holy Orders. The major purpose of the amendment is also shown here. §§ 4-8 deal with the changes in canons related to the sacrament of marriage. The remaining text of Motu Proprio consists of the modified canons, replacing previous legal-canonical texts, in the Code of Canon Law. Finally, venerable Pope Benedict XVI orders the Motu Proprio to be published in the official qazette "Acta Apostolicae Sedis" to have the force of law.

After the introductory remarks above, I'd like to touch upon the structure of this essay. ***Section 1*** has been dedicated to brief comparative analysis of secular legal and Canon Law norm-creation systems. ***Section 2*** analyses a special status of the Church. The first amendment in Motu Proprio with regards to the changes to canons on the Sacrament of Holy Orders is analysed in ***section 3*** of this essay. Finally, before coming up with appropriate conclusions, ***section 4*** looks into the details of the second amendment to canons on the sacrament of marriage. As the last point, a list of the used literature and sources is attached to the essay.

General remarks on norm-creation/revision: secular legal systems and Canon Law

In modern world historic ties between the divine law and secular law[1] seems broken today, as a result of many revolutionary currents of thought, which deepened, systematised and maximised the practical use of human knowledge. Atheism, science, secularism etc.[2] are apparently the major elements giving birth to the proper theological foundations which have become serious challengers to the religion.

Nowadays, *"the law is a social process, a living thing for recognising and marshalling the values"*[3] in any secular legal system. And in many European democracies the religion has been placed within the limits of the concept of Freedom

---

[1] Law and Revolution: the Formation of Western Legal Tradition, Harold J.Berman, printed in the USA, 1983, pp.275
[2] Mike King, *"Secularism: the Hidden Origins of Disbelief"*, Cambridge, 2007; Karen Armstrong, *"The Case for God: What Religion Really Means"*, London, 2009.
[3] Brian Dickson, *"A Life in the Law: The Process of Judging"*, 63 Sask. L. Rev., (2000) p.388

of Religion and Belief[1] under the umbrella of Human Rights Law. Also, Rabbi Burton L. Visotzky, discussing the situation in the USA, states that *"The result of a marriage of "divine law" with our "secular society" would be a form of "tyranny of the majority"*[2].

Under such circumstances, a commonly accepted view is that *"the legislative bodies in the secular legal systems have the full authority to change the law created by themselves in order to encompass the new social reality"*.[3] For this purpose the emergence of some preconditions will be sufficient (changing values in society, advances in technology etc.)[4].

This picture changes completely in case of unchangeable religious legal systems. Canon Law is also religious law[5], and *"its nature and functions are predominantly theological"*.[6] The Church *"performs a mission received from God, it preaches the Gospel to all which is unchangeable"*.[7] However, Canon Law has a very unique and adequate attitude towards such kind of "stability". Changes are necessary in it, as *"an informed conscience takes precedence over law"*.[8]

Canon Law has changed over the centuries. As an example, one can mention differences between the 1917 and 1983 Codes. The major ones include *a reduction of the number of laws* (from 2,414 to 1752), *a shift in the "spirit" of law* (in the 1983 Code the purpose of the Canon Law is "salus animarum"), *an enhance-*

---

[1] EU Guidelines on the promotion and protection of freedom of religion and belief, 24 June 2013, available at: http://eu-un.europa.eu/articles/en/article_13685_en.htm

[2] DePaul Law Review, Volume 51, Issue 4 (Summer 2002), Article 5, pp. 1061-1076, *"The Myth of Divine Law in Secular Society"*, by Rabbi Burton L. Visotzky p.1075.

[3] Aharon Barak, "The Judge in a Democracy", Princeton University Press, 2006, summary of the book, p.4. Available at: http://press.princeton.edu/chapters/s8145.pdf

[4] http://lib.oup.com.au/secondary/legal_studies/justice_and_outcomes/Justice-and-Outcomes-ch2-Law-making-through-parliament.pdf

[5] For example, see article titled "The Origins of Church Law" by Raymond F.Collins in: The Jurist 61 (2001), 134-156.

[6] Ecclesiastical Law Journal, Volume 14, Issue 02, May 2012, pp 164-194, *"Canon Law and Theology"*, by Robert Ombres, p. 193

[7] Second Vatican Council, *Gaudium et Spes*, 7 December 1965, No 89.

[8] Thomas Aquinas, Summa Theologica, First Part of the Second Part, Question 97

ment of theological context (theological contexts are given within legal parameters), *a reaffirmation of the equality of all Christians*.[1] This all apparently happened due to the specific status of the Church in the norm creation/revision.

The special status of the Church in law creation

The documents of Vatican I and Vatican II see the Church as a perfect society[2], as an assembly of the faithful of Christ and a true society[3], as a kind of sacrament of intimate union with God and of the unity of whole human race[4], kingdom of Christ which grows visibly through the power of God[5]. Thus, an institution with such a divine status must have all capacity to establish legal rules, to revise them and to make necessary amendments.

The Church is also "a living organism, designed to function very much like the human body".[6] In other words, the Church is an earthly, social, visible institution, uniting the Christian faithful physically.[7]

The first amendment – the diaconate in the Holy Order

Amendment to canons 1008 and 1009 originates from the CCC n. 1581, which in its turn, is based on n. 29 of the Dogmatic Constitution Lumen Gentium. § 1 of n. 29 details the major functions attributed to deacons (for instance, to administer baptism, to be custodian and dispenser of the Eucharist etc.). Its § 2 has a prospective function. It establishes a precondition for the future in relation to

---

[1] http://www.dummies.com/how-to/content/revising-the-code-of-canon-law-1983.html
[2] Primum schema constitution de ecclesia Christi, 1870, § 10
[3] Schema constitutionis dogmaticae secundae de ecclesia Christi secundum reverendissimorum patrum animadversiones reformatum, 1870, § 2
[4] Dogmatic Constitution on the Church Lumen Gentium, 1964, § 1
[5] Dogmatic Constitution on the Church Lumen Gentium, 1964, § 3
[6] Ephesians 4:15
[7] Apostolic Constitution Sacrae Disciplinae Leges of 1983. See the Code of Canon Law, Latin-English Edition 2012, page xxxi.

the restoration of the diaconate as *"a permanent rank of the hierarchy"*, as the duties of deacons, listed in § 1 are *"very necessary for the life of the Church"*. The competence to make a decision on this issue, subject to the approval by the Supreme Pontiff, is attributed to the territorial bodies of bishops. Under § 2, such kind of diaconate can, in the future, be conferred upon mature men living in the married status and young men subject to the conditions of the law of celibacy.

In other words, second edition of n. 1581 of the CCC contains the provisions modified in the lights of n. 29 of Lumen Gentium which seek to avoid extending to the grade of deacon the ability to act in *persona Christi Capitis*. This amendment was approved by John Paul II in 1998 and he also mandated the adjustment of the appropriate canons in the Code of Canon Law.

Thus, previous versions of canons 1008 and 1009 contained different wording.[1] The major change in canon 1008 is that it does no longer state that the sacrament confers the faculty of acting in the person of Christ the Head and attributes a specific title to those who receive the Sacrament of Orders to serve the People of God. What about canon 1009, the major newness is the inclusion of § 3 which serves the goal of drawing a clear line between the sphere of activities of three "Holy Orders"[2]. Thus, episcopate and presbyterate *"...receive the mission and capacity to act in the person of Christ the Head..."*, whereas *"deacons are empowered to serve the People of God in the ministries of liturgy, the word and charity"*.[3]

To summarise this section, I would like, to introduce a distinction between the deacons and other two ministries. Commonly accepted canonical view is that deacons aren't ordained to the "priesthood", but to the "ministry". The deacon represents Christ, not as High Priest, but as the one who came "not be to served,

---

[1] Available at: http://www.intratext.com/IXT/ENG0017/_P3M.HTM

[2] For details see : http://www.newadvent.org/cathen/11279a.htm

[3] Dogmatic Constitution on the Church Lumen Gentium (1964), nn. 27, 28, 29 respectively; Catechism of the Catholic Church (1992) §§ 1555-1561, 1562-1568, 1569-1571 respectively.

but to serve. The priest and the deacon are united through their ordination with the bishop, and the latter as the bishop's helper in many different kinds of diakonia, ministry to the poor, of the Word, at the altar."[1]

The second amendment – subordinate clause "and has not left it by a formal act"

The suppression of a subordinate clause in three canons concerning marriage was the second major task of the Motu Proprio. Because the normative (legal) requirement contained in the clause *"and has not left it by a formal act"* did not find necessary support in its practical application. The main purpose of the clause in previous versions of canons 1086 § 1 (the impediment of disparity of cult), 1117 (canonical form of marriage) and 1124 (need for permission in case of mixed marriages) of the Code was to facilitate the application of the *ius connubii* for certain people separated from the Church. The formula excluded all such people from the general rule of Canon 11 due to the fact that it was not possible for them in reality to be able to follow the provisions of the Code on the form of the celebration of marriage. In other words, it aimed at avoiding the situations in which the marriages contracted by the estranged faithful could become invalid due to defect of form or impediment of disparity of cult.

However, there were a lot of practical difficulties in many areas related to the interpretation and application of the formula mentioned above. **Firstly**, in practice it was, both theologically and canonically, too difficult to determine what the act of separation from the Church had meant. **Secondly**, the new law embodied in the formula gave birth to many pastoral problems (e.g., facilitating apostasy in places where the number of Catholics was relatively few, and where discriminative marriage laws were in force). **Thirdly**, the new law also closed the return

---

[1] Christoph Schönborn, Living the Catechism of the Catholic Church, Volume 2, "The Sacraments", Vienna, 1996, p.47

doors for the baptized persons who, failing previous marriage, was willing to contract a new, canonical one. **Fourthly**, many of the "excluded marriages" became "clandestine marriages".[1]

The issue was first considered by the Pontifical Council for the Interpretation of Legislative Texts. The Plenary Session of 3 June 1997 approved the formulation of a *dubium* and the relative *responsum*[2] in order to provide for an authentic interpretation of the precise legal meaning of the clause. Then the process of consulting the Bishops' Conferences took place for the next two years. As a result, two major actions to be taken were singled out: clarifying the precise meaning of the phrase; eliminating it completely. Another Plenary Session of the Pontifical Council held on 4 June 1999 unanimously approved the proposal to eliminate the clause above. The then Supreme Pontiff confirmed this decision in the Audience of 3 July 1999 and ordered to start the drafting of the appropriate texts.[3]

Since the entrance into force of the Code in 1983, if any Catholic made a formal act of abandoning the Catholic Church, he or she was not bound to all appropriate canons. The Motu Proprio changed this practice by the suppression of the clause in all three canons and canon 11 regained its force with respect to all persons referred to in the previous sentence.

Conclusions

The discussions carried out in the previous sections of this essay demonstrate the fact that Canon Law possesses perfect law revision mechanisms. Despite the fact that the unchangeable Divine Law remains as one of the major sources, Canon

---

[1] "On *Omnium in Mentem*: The Basis of the Two Changes" by Archbishop Francesco Coccopalmerio, 2010. Available at: http://www.ewtn.com/library/CANONLAW/bas2changes.htm

[2] Responsum ad Dubium – response to the doubt. It is a formal response given by the appropriate authority to a question raised about the meaning or interpretation of a certain point. See: Consecrated Phrases: A Latin Theological Dictionary: Latin expressions commonly found in theological writings, by James T.Bretzke, third edition, Minnesota, 2013, , p.211

[3] "On *Omnium in Mentem*: The Basis of the Two Changes" by Archbishop Francesco Coccopalmerio, 2010. Available at: http://www.ewtn.com/library/CANONLAW/bas2changes.htm

Law is functioning in both legal and theological ways very effectively to respond to the challenges of contemporary ages. This unique task is successfully implemented due to the dual status of the Church in the world: she maintains her spirituality; she acts as a visible, social structure.

Motu Proprio emerged as a result of the implementation of the law revision function of the Church as a visible structure, in order to bring the unsuitable rules in line with the commonly accepted practices. The first amendment proclaims we have to define the meaning of ordination not in terms of doing, of function, but first of all in terms of being[1]. It draws a line between three Holy Orders and attributes a specific title to those who receive the Sacrament of Orders.

Furthermore, Motu Proprio suppressed the clause on "formal act" in three canons on marriage with its second amendment which proved itself to be inadequate and unsuitable in practice. This apparently had positive practical effects on the Church Administration and Community by resolving many pastoral and other practical problems, by keeping the doors of the Church open for all in the context of the subject-matter of this essay, and by minimising the possibility of "clandestine marriages".

Before concluding, I would like to underline one more point. In my humble opinion, Motu Proprio has a well-established connection with the canonical doctrine of reception. New rules discussed above were introduced as the law which did not prove to be acceptable in their practical application. The Church took all necessary measures to withdrew them and introduce more applicable ones. This proves the fact that *the ancient doctrine of reception of canonical rules by the communities is still an honourable part of Catholic tradition*[2].

---

[1] Christoph Schönborn, Living the Catechism of the Catholic Church, Volume 2, "The Sacraments", Vienna, 1996, p.47

[2] The Jurist 50 (1990) 58-82, The Canonical Doctrine of Reception, James A. Coriden, p.72

Bibliography

Literature/Articles

1/ R.H. Helmholz, The Spirit of Classical Canon Law, Paperback edition 2010.
2/ Law and Revolution: the Formation of Western Legal Tradition, Harold J.Berman, printed in the USA, 1983.
3/ Robert Somerville, "*Canon Law, Religion and Politics*", Catholic University of America Press, 2012.
4/ Mike King, "*Secularism: the Hidden Origins of Disbelief*", Cambridge, 2007.
5/ Karen Armstrong, "*The Case for God: What Religion Really Means*", London, 2009.
6/ Aharon Barak, "The Judge in a Democracy", Princeton University Press, 2006, summary of the book.
7/ "The Origins of Church Law" by Raymond F.Collins in: The Jurist 61 (2001).
8/ Brian Dickson, "*A Life in the Law: The Process of Judging*", 63 Sask. L. Rev., 2000.
"*Canon Law as a Religious Legal System*", by Silvio Ferrari, pp. 49-60.in the book "*Religion Law and Tradition: Comparative Studies in Religious Law*", edited by Andrew Huxley, New York, 2002.
9/ DePaul Law Review, Volume 51, Issue 4 (Summer 2002), Article 5, pp. 1061-1076, "*The Myth of Divine Law in Secular Society*", by Rabbi Burton L. Visotzky p.1075.
10/ Ecclesiastical Law Journal, Volume 14, Issue 02, May 2012, pp 164-194, "*Canon Law and Theology*", by Robert Ombres.
11/ Christoph Schönborn, Living the Catechism of the Catholic Church, Volume 2, "The Sacraments", Vienna, 1996.
12/ "On *Omnium in Mentem*: The Basis of the Two Changes" by Archbishop Francesco Coccopalmerio, 2010.
13/ Thomas Aquinas, Summa Theologica, First Part of the Second Part, Question 97
14/ The Jurist 50 (1990) 58-82, The Canonical Doctrine of Reception, James A. Coriden

Canon Law Documents

1/ Primum schema constitution de ecclesia Christi, 1870.
2/ Schema constitutionis dogmaticae secundae de ecclesia Christi secundum reverendissimorum patrum animadversiones reformatum, 1870.

3/ Dogmatic Constitution on the Church Lumen Gentium, 1964.
4/ Second Vatican Council, *Gaudium et Spes*, 7 December 1965.
5/ Apostolic Constitution Sacrae Disciplinae Leges of 1983.
6/ Catechism of the Catholic Church, 1992.

International/Domestic Legal Acts

1/ EU Guidelines on the promotion and protection of freedom of religion and belief, 24 June 2013

Websites

http://eu-un.europa.eu/articles/en/article_13685_en.htm
http://press.princeton.edu/chapters/s8145.pdf
http://lib.oup.com.au/secondary/legal_studies/justice_and_outcomes/Justice-and-Outcomes-ch2-Law-making-through-parliament.pdf
http://www.intratext.com/IXT/ENG0017/_P3M.HTM
http://www.newadvent.org/cathen/11279a.htm
http://www.ewtn.com/library/CANONLAW/bas2changes.htm
http://www.ewtn.com/library/CANONLAW/bas2changes.htm
http://www.dummies.com/how-to/content/revising-the-code-of-canon-law-1983.html

Dictionaries

Consecrated Phrases: A Latin Theological Dictionary: Latin expressions commonly found in theological writings, by James T.Bretzke, third edition, Minnesota, 2013.

Essay No 3. 'The Canonical Doctrine of Reception' by James Coriden

Keywords: *The canonical doctrine of reception.*

Introduction

The article titled "The Canonical Doctrine of Reception" by distinguished canonist, Dr James A. Coriden has been selected as a major topic of the current essay. The main issue dealt with by the author, as can be implied from the title, is the problem of reception of new canonical rules by the respective communities. But before getting into details of the article, I would like to touch upon four general functions of law which are, by analogy, according to another work of the same author, applicable to canonical rules and include: to help the society to achieve its goals; to afford stability and good order to the society; to protect personal rights; to assist in the education of the community[1]. These functions constitute a set of helpful arguments which increase the strength of the doctrine of reception.

Thus, Dr. James Coriden starts his article with his analysis on the origins, sources and authors of the doctrine, discusses its pros and cons, formulates some definitions, scrutinises the Code of Canon Law and advises appropriate canons to be taken into consideration, examines theological foundations of the conception, looks into the practical applications of it, and finally arrives at several conclusions. The interpretation of his very first sentence brings us to the conclusion that *any believing community can be effectively guided only by those laws and rules which have been truly and voluntarily accepted by the same community.* This major argument is quite well-structured in the article by the use of proper

---

[1] James A. Coriden, An Introduction to Canon Law, Paulist Press, New York, 1991, pp. 5-6

research methods and references to a series of important studies[1]. The brief introductory part comes to the end with the closing paragraph in which the author draws a map of his work in order to supply the readers with necessary information about the structure of the article.

Accordingly, the 24 pages article is divided into eight sections given under the capital letters of Latin alphabet from A to H (including H). Some sections are also divided into appropriate sub-sections which come under Roman numerals. Also, the article has a non-titled introductory part consisting of several paragraphs and closing remarks of the author are contained in the last section titled 'Conclusion'.

II. Any new rule has to be accepted by the community in order to become an effective guide!

The title of the current section of this essay is a reflection of the major argument deriving from the very first sentence of Dr. Coriden's article. And *sections A, B, C and D are very important from the perspective of building the above argument up, supporting it with various elements, and proving its credibility. Thus, section A, titled "Presuppositions"* contains provisions on the *major dissimimilitudo* between canonical rules and secular laws. So, the Church is different from the state in origin, purpose, history etc., the purpose of canonical rules is *salus animarum*, the sources of authority are the power of the Risen Lord. As the spirit of God is present and operative in each of the members of the community of faith, all have something to say about its faith and its discipline (pages 59-60).

In Section B, the author looks into the origins of the doctrine and notes that it is rooted in the works of Augustine of Hippo, Isidore of Seville, Augustine, and

---

[1] He provides citations of the appropriate works by prominent scholars like Luigi DeLuca, Yves Congar, Hubert Müller, Brian Tierney, Geoffrey King, Richard Potz, Peter Leisching and Werner Kramer.

John Gratian[1]. Then he quotes the Decretum: *"Laws are instituted with promulgation and are more firmly established when they are approved by the practices of those who observe them"* and correlatively, a law can be invalidated simply by being ignored"[2]. He further mentions Isidore's well-known description of the necessary qualities of law (a law will be moral, just etc.)[3]. Dr. Coriden focuses on the rule-making as a two-step process: *in the first stage a legitimate ecclesiastical authority sets forth the law, and in the second stage, the subjects either approve or withhold their approval.*

Dr. Coriden provides another set of supportive ideas for his argument in section C (Proponents) by quoting various authors who represented various schools of thought (conciliarists[4], Gallicans[5], Febronians[6], Jansenits[7], monarchists and papal absolutists) in pages 63-69. For instance, decretists considered that for any law to become binding, the substantive content of it would be in accord with the divine truth and the church had to receipt that law. Then he mentions Glossa Palatina which separates *de iure* and *de facto* confirmation of law[8]. The author quotes Matthaeus Romanus[9] who taught that acceptance is one of the three (institution, promulgation) requirements for a law to become obligatory. Additionally, the author considers the appropriate ideas of XIV-XIX century canonists who contributed to the doctrine of reception. *And in section D, pages 69-71, the author provides summarised comments* on the thoughts discussed in the previous section.

---

[1] The Jurist 50 (1990) 58-82, The Canonical Doctrine of Reception, James A. Coriden, p.58

[2] Decretum (circa 1140), Distinction 4, canon 3.

[3] "The Etymologies of Isidore of Seville, translated by Stephen A. Barney, W.J. Lewis, J.A. Beach, Oliver Berghof, Cambridge University Press, 2006. In particular, please see Book V, "Law and Times", pages 117-135.

[4] http://www.catholicculture.org/culture/library/dictionary/index.cfm?id=32689

[5] Jotham Parsons, The Church in the Republic: Gallicanism and Political Ideology in Renaissance France, Catholic University of America Press, 2004, pp. 14–51.

[6] William H. Brackney, Historical Dictionary of Radical Christianity, Lanham, Maryland 2012, pp. 124-125.

[7] http://www.britannica.com/EBchecked/topic/300421/Jansenism

[8] Glossia Palatina ad Dist. 19 c. 9: "it would be too dangerous to entrust our faith to the judgment [or will] of a single man".

[9] The Dissertation by Tobias Speck in German titled "Quod omnes tangit: Rezeption als ekklesiologisches Phänomen bei Matthäus Romanus und Wilhelm von Ockham", 16 Juli, 2009. Available at: http://www.freidok.uni-freiburg.de/volltexte/6936/pdf/DissertationSpeck2009.pdf

In next three sections Dr. Coriden discusses further elements to prove his argument by weighing several counter-arguments, interrogating some aspects of the doctrine, and addressing the theological origins of it. For example, *Section E displays the atmosphere of confrontations between the Holy See and Gallicans* in which the doctrine of reception was somehow affected by the 1665 condemnation act of the Inquisition (28 propositions were censured)[1]. *Section F follows with the effort to find answers to several questions* ("is acceptance by people required?" and "who are the users or people?" etc.). In pages 73-75, the author distinguishes the process of establishing a rule *in actu primo* or *de iure* and *in actu secundo* or *de facto*. The definition of law given by Thomas Aquinas, as an ordination of reason, is quoted in order to provide one more argument in favour of the doctrine of reception[2]. A particular attention is paid to the proper canons in the Code of Canon Law which are related to and supportive of the reception (Canons 7, 25, canons on marriage). However, the author underlines several concepts which are considered different from reception: e.g., contrary customs abrogate the law; rebellious disobedience or disregards for rightful authority.

Section G contains pure theological foundations of the doctrine which encompass such concepts like "sharing the life and mission of the Church", "God is dwelling within each one of the faithful", "Christ is present ... in gatherings of his believers", "true equality among the members of the Church" etc. *And Section H covers some practical issues related to the application of the principle of reception.* Those include regulations from two popes (Telesphous and Gregory) for fast and abstinence for clerics at certain times of the liturgical year, the doctrine of a "Truce of God"[3], fasting from chees and eggs, holding provincial council

---

[1] The Jurist 50 (1990) 58-82, The Canonical Doctrine of Reception, James A. Coriden, p.72
[2] Thomas Aquinas, Contemporary Philosophical Perspectives, edited by Brian Davies, Oxford University Press, 2002, pp. 325-339
[3] Theological Dictionary, by Charles Buck, two volumes in one, Philadelphia, 1815, p. 508

every twenty years, use of Latin for teaching in seminaries and other church institutions (Veterum Sapientia) etc. The author adds that in vastly more numerous instances the doctrine played an important role.

In the "Conclusions", the author records that rule-making has substantive and formal *elements*. He is of the opinion that medieval doctrine of reception (*any law should be consonant with the Scriptures, traditions and truth*) was in better condition than the modern. Dr. Coriden singles out three reasons for that. *First*, he considers that the above-mentioned 1665 condemnation cast the doctrine into a shadow. *Second*, schools like Voluntarism[1] and Rationalism[2] are also the causes of the current situation. *Third*, the claim that Church authority resides exclusively in the office-holder is seen as another reason. Despite a little bit pessimistic concluding tone, *the author finally considers the reception of canonical rules by the communities as an ancient and honourable part of Catholic tradition.*

III. Perspectives of the doctrine of reception in modern ages

The article encompasses many aspects of the doctrine of reception very successfully. However one of those aspects seems, in my humble opinion, more challenging. It is related to the modern attitudes towards the doctrine. It would really be interesting to get into more details and determine the current position of the doctrine. In particular, I would like to look at several aspects of the problem in more detail and try to answer the question why the doctrine has lost much of its Medieval Ages reputation nowadays?

The analysis can be carried out from the point of view of relationships between the church and state authorities, church and science, church and secular communities, church and other religious and non-religious communities etc. A

---

[1] Roger Crisp, The Oxford Handbook of the History of Ethics, Oxford, United Kingdom, 2013, pp.221-222
[2] Modern Law Review, Volume 76, Issue 4, Rationalism in Public Law, by Graham Gee and Gregoire Webber, pp. 708-734.

particular attention might be paid to modern implications of two opposite doctrines: the doctrine of reception and the doctrine of imposition. In addition, it seems appropriate to study examples of application of the doctrine in the secular legal system of various countries. For instance, one of those examples might be the Caribbean Jurisdictions[1].

Alongside with the national secular legal systems, the place and role of the doctrine of reception in international law and European Union law can be briefly taken into consideration as well. Because contemporary ages are very multidimensional, full of challenges and threats. These factors of utmost importance increase the significance of the effective legal regulation. Of course, the importance of canonical rules as one of the major regulative elements is undeniable[2]. However multidimensional approach might be fit-for-purpose in proceeding any further research activities.

I would like to conclude this essay with several points relating to my preferences in choosing this topic. *First of all*, it is a very topical question with a very important agenda. *Secondly*, contemporary societies are primarily subject to the imposition doctrine and I am wondering if there can be further possibilities for the doctrine of reception. *Thirdly*, I conceive the more widely application of the doctrine of reception as one of the effective preventive means in conflict resolution within modern societies.

At this point it seems necessary to comment on the above points briefly in order to analyse further possibilities that the doctrine of reception could have in contemporary ages. Thus, the doctrine of reception seems to have focused on a certain degree of freedoms and liberties granted to the communities in the past. To some extent, it was in a dual relationships with the customs. Sometimes it was on the same front with the customs of the communities protecting the internal,

---

[1] Rose-Marie Belle Antoine, Commonwealth Caribbean Law and Legal Systems, second edition, New York 2008, Chapter 5, pp. 73-93

[2] Apostolic Constitution Sacrae Disciplinae Leges of 1983. See the Code of Canon Law, Latin-English Edition, 2012, page xxxi

working practices against new, external rules. But at times, the doctrine did probably have negative impacts on the society while it could also fight for the customary rules of the communities which were in total contradiction with the principles and rules of the, for example, Divine Law. Today this rivalry is still actual, despite the fact that the third external element, namely, interventions of the secular front by the use of the imposition doctrine have also tremendous impacts on the communities.

In my humble opinion, the historical beneficiaries of this doctrine, as a rule, were not individuals but large collectives of individuals united in the religious communities. In other words, the will of majority prevailed in cases of conflict between two confronting rules. Nowadays, there are several issues to be singled out on this context. *First*, the idea of human rights and freedoms are becoming more and more individualistic. It would be interesting to know whether habits of an individual can be considered as "the custom/s" which would give this specific individual the right to reject a rule imposed contrary to his this or that habit. For example, there are ongoing tense debates on a set of rights of the individuals which allegedly allows them to be able to make exceptions for themselves to the generally accepted rules (e.g., to refuse to join the army on the basis of religious thoughts).

On the other side, the religious communities are in a very close interaction with other religious, secular, non-religious communities. Communities can also be national, local regional, global, political, legal etc. This classification is characterised with many overlapping elements, of course. However the activities of each of them are regulated by the application of a set of rules which are different in origin, nature and, and source. For example, the practices of the non-religious communities do totally exclude religious norms. Therefore it seems very intriguing to have detailed investigations in order to find out whether the doctrine of appreciation can be applied to such situations in which any of the confronting communities, mentioned in the introduction to this paragraph, is legally allowed to exclude rules imposed by its rivals. The brightest example might be the perspectives of the application of the norms of international law to the various domestic political communities.

Last but not least, I would love to apply this canonical doctrine to a complex set of contemporary inter-community relationships. Because, as obvious, these relationships also play a dual role. Namely, they may develop/progress the societies/communities in a positive way, so that humankind can continue, for example, to explore the outer-space more successfully; or they may bring one, several or all of those communities to the edge of tragedies, catastrophes and self-destruction. From this point of view, the thorough examination of the doctrine of reception seems to me extraordinarily important, as it can be a source of conflicts or a source of the resolution of conflicts.

Bibliography

1. James A. Coriden, An Introduction to Canon Law, Paulist Press, New York, 1991
2. The Jurist 50 (1990) 58-82, The Canonical Doctrine of Reception, James A. Coriden
3. Decretum (circa 1140)
4. Glossia Palatina ad Dist. 19 c. 9
5. "The Etymologies of Isidore of Seville, translated by Stephen A. Barney, W.J. Lewis, J.A. Beach, Oliver Berghof, Cambrige University Press, 2006.
6. Jotham Parsons, The Church in the Republic: Gallicanism and Political Ideology in Renaissance France, Catholic University of America Press, 2004
7. William H. Brackney, Historical Dictionary of Radical Christianity, Lanham, Maryland
8. Thomas Aquinas, Contemporary Philosophical Perspectives, edited by Brian Davies, Oxford University Press, 2002
9. Theological Dictionary, by Charles Buck, two volumes in one, Philadelphia, 1815
10. Roger Crisp, The Oxford Handbook of the History of Ethics, Oxford, United Kingdom, 2013
11. Modern Law Review, Volume 76, Issue 4, Rationalism in Public Law, by Graham Gee and Gregoire Webber, pp. 708-734
12. Rose-Marie Belle Antoine, Commonwealth Caribbean Law and Legal Systems, second edition, New York 2008
13. Apostolic Constitution Sacrae Disciplinae Leges of 1983. See the Code of Canon Law, Latin-English Edition, 2012
14. Code of Canon Law (1983)
15. http://www.catholicculture.org/culture/library/dictionary/index.cfm?id=32689
16. http://www.britannica.com/EBchecked/topic/300421/Jansenism
17. http://www.freidok.uni-freiburg.de/volltexte/6936/pdf/DissertationSpeck2009.pdf

Essay No 4. CASE OF ISLAM-ITTIHAD ASSOCIATION V. AZERBAIJAN REPUBLIC

Keywords: *Freedom of religion and belief; case law; European Court on Human Rights; Islam-Ittihad and others v. Azerbaijan.*

Introduction

Islam-Ittihad and others v. Azerbaijan ("the Case")[1] is one of the most recent cases seen by the European Court of Human Rights ("the Court"). It was lodged with the Court on 17 January 2005. Two Azerbaijani nationals appealed against the Azerbaijani Government. The Court in its 13 November 2014 judgement unanimously held that there had been a violation of Article 11.

The above paragraph constitutes a very brief survey of the case. It does not seem to be a pure freedom of religion and belief (FORB) issue. Nevertheless, the details of the case prove that the freedom of association in this particular context has been closely linked to the religious activities.

Now I would like to provide a brief overview of the structure of the article. The next section has been dedicated to the details of the case. Secondly, the doctrinal issues and case law of the Court will be analysed in order to reach the middle ground between universal values and local necessities. Thirdly, Azerbaijan-specific FORB environments will be discussed. Lastly, the major outcomes of the analysis and discussions carried out in the essay will be put in the conclusory findings.

---

[1] *For the online version of the case please http://hudoc.echr.coe.int/sites/eng/pages/search.aspx?i=001-147866#{"itemid":["001-147866"]}*

Details of the Case: Agenda and activities of the Association, domestic legislation and the Court findings

Azerbaijan was a highly secular society before the collapse of the USSR. This dissolution gave birth to the spread of Islam in the territory of CIS republics[1], including Azerbaijan. The 1995 Constitution clearly establishes country as a "democratic, legal, secular and unitary republic"[2]. However, since 1991 several denominations of Islam has entered into competition with secularism.

The Islam-Ittihad[3] Association was also established in 1991. The Ministry of Justice ("the Ministry") of AR registered it in 1995. Its main aims included "the repair and maintenance of abandoned mosques and other places of worship, organising pilgrimages to Islamic shrines, providing material and moral aid to orphanages as well as elderly, ill and disabled people, and publishing books with a religious content" (§ 9 of the Judgement). And its actual activities encompassed the repair of some religious buildings, the provision of financial assistance to the people in need, the propagation of the historical and religious values, and publishing appropriate articles in the media.

Nevertheless, inspections of the Association's activities by the Ministry in 2002 discovered several nonconformities between the allowed and actual actions. *The Association did not have a bank account, the sources of financing were not clear, there were no accounting records, its actual headquarters were located in a mosque. Also, the chairman and members of the Association belonged to the same religious community[4]. More importantly, the Ministry claimed that the Association's actual primary activities involved religious propaganda and agitation which was acknowledged as being totally unlawful (§§ 11-16).*

---

[1] *Galina Yemelianova, Radical Islam in the Former Soviet Union, chapter 6 (2010)*
[2] *The 1995 Constitution of Azerbaijan Republic, Article 7, item 1*
[3] *The Arabic word "ittihad" means "union", or "unification"*
[4] *Galina Yemelianova, pp. 185-186*

After exchange of correspondence between the parties, on 2 July 2003 the Ministry lodged an action with a District Court which found that *"the Association had unlawfully engaged in religious activities and, despite three warnings by the Ministry, had failed to take any measure to cease such activities"* (§ 22). The Association was dissolved on 28 August 2003.

The Association claimed that *"the Ministry had failed to specify which of the Association's activities was qualified as "religious activity"*, *"Azerbaijani legislation did not provide any precise definition of what constituted a "religious activity"* (§ 17) and *"the first instance court had put the burden of proof on it"* (§ 23). But on 20 November 2003 the Court of Appeal and on 21 July 2004 the Supreme Court upheld decisions of the previous instances.

The applicants took the case to the Court claiming that the forced dissolution of the Association had violated their rights to freedom of expression and freedom of association. The major findings of the Court solely on Article 11 include:

1. The sanction imposed on the Association had a basis in domestic law and the law was accessible (§ 45);
2. Domestic courts based the dissolution of the Association on the fact that it had engaged in religious activities, despite the fact that it had the status of a non-governmental organisations (§ 48);
3. The Azerbaijani law, as in force at the material time, did not provide any definition of what constituted *"professional religious activity"* (§§ 47-48)[1] and this made it impossible to foresee what constituted *"religious activity"*;
4. Moreover, the Ministry and domestic courts, instead of giving an interpretation of *"religious activity"*, and legally proving which activities of the Association were exactly *"religious"*, strikingly, imposed the burden of proof on the Association (49);

---

[1] See also: *Seyidzade v. Azerbaijan*, no. 37700/05, §§ 31-40 (3 December 2009)

5. Clause 2 of the 1995 Charter of the Association contained provisions related to the organisation of pilgrimages to holy shrines, and if this kind of activity was to be considered *"religious"*, then the Ministry had omitted to request the Association to amend those provision (§ 50).

Additionally, the Court rejected the alleged violation of Article 6 of the Convention (reasonable time requirement), as it could not find any proof of this claim among the materials in its possession (§§ 53-54). Apparently, on the basis of stronger legal arguments, the Court found violation of Article 11 and held unanimously that the respondent State had to pay the applicants, within three months from the date on which the judgement becomes final, 4,000 Euro in respect of non-pecuniary damage and 2,000 Euro in respect of costs and expenses.

Striking balance between the national interests and universal values: a legal necessity or a legal circumvention

The decision of the Court is to become final in the circumstances set out in Article 44 § 2 of the Convention and the attitude of all judges reserves due respect. However, a "legal conflict between two parties + a fundamental human right to be protected + unsuccessful domestic courts + a helpful cross-border Court = solution" formula seems to be only a visible side of the iceberg in this case. There are also religious, social, economic, political, even geopolitical aspects of the problem. Certainly, those aspects gave birth to this legal conflict, and undoubtedly, had serious impact on its resolution at the domestic level.

Many distinguished Western scholars are well-familiar with the mentioned aspects[1]. They are not vague claims used to circumvent international legal obligations of a state. There are real threats which require striking an adequate and necessary balance between secularism and religiosity. The notion *"striking balance"*

---

[1] *Willy Fautré, Non-Muslim Minorities in Azerbaijan: From Their First Inception through Russian Empire and Soviet Repression to Present-Day Secular State of Azerbaijan, Conclusions, § 3 (October 2013)*. Online version is available at: www.academia.edu/5201189/Non-Muslim_Minorities_in_Azerbaijan_a_Secular_State

in this context is not something new at all and it does not denote to the legal circumvention. The Court has a *"margin of appreciation"* doctrine which is understood as *"the latitude of deference or error which the Strasbourg organs will allow to national legislative, executive, administrative and judicial bodies"*[1]. The major aim of this doctrine is *"to strike a balance between national views of human rights and the uniform application of Convention values"*[2].

This doctrine[3] is a comprehensive legal tool with the well-established principles consisting of effective protection[4], subsidiarity[5] and review, permissible interference with Convention rights (prescribed by law and in accordance with law; legitimate aims; necessary in a democratic society), proportionality[6], and the "European Consensus" standard[7]. Moreover, there is a growing tendency of its application in international law in general[8] and in international case law[9].

Briefly speaking, *"The needs and resources of the community and individuals has to be given due regard while ensuring compliance with the Convention. In that, the Contracting States enjoy a wide margin of appreciation"*[10]. And what are those needs and necessities of the Azerbaijani society with secular majority today? The next section may be helpful to find appropriate answers to this question.

---

[1] *Howard Charles Yourow, The Margin of Appreciation Doctrine in the Dynamics of European Human Rights Jurisprudence, p.13 (1996)*

[2] *Yutaka Arai-Takahashi, The Margin of Appreciation Doctrine and the Principle of Proportionality in the Jurisprudence of ECHR, p.3 (2001)*

[3] Please see: www.coe.int/t/dghl/cooperation/lisbonnetwork/Themis/ECHR/Paper2_en.asp#P65_400

[4] *Bernadette Rainey, Concentrate Human Rights Law, p. 142 (2nd ed. 2013)*

[5] *Paolo G. Carozza, Subsidiarity as a Structural Principle of International Human Rights Law, 97 The American Journal of International Law, pp.38-79, (Jan., 2003)*

[6] *Jeremy McBride, "Proportionality and the European Convention on Human Rights" in the book: Evelin Ellis, The Principle of Proportionality in the Laws of Europe, pp.23-37 (1999)*

[7] *Rasmussen v. Denmark, No.8777/79, § 40 (28 Nov., 1984) and Sunday Times v. United Kingdom, no.6538/74, § 59 (26 Apr. 1979).*

[8] *Yuval Shany, Toward a General Margin of Appreciation Doctrine in International Law, 16 The European Journal of International Law, p.908 (2006)*

[9] Three ICJ cases including "Oil Platforms", "Avena" (only this case embraced the possibility of the use of the doctrine), and "Wall in the Occupied Palestinian Territory"

[10] *Lautsi and others v. Italy, no.30814/16, § 61 (18 March 2011)*

Factors affecting FORB environments in Azerbaijan positively and negatively

There are several major factors to be discussed in this section. *First of all*, for centuries Azerbaijan has been a land of clashes and dialogues between several faiths and religions[1]. Subsequently, this centuries-old and persistent, even though sometimes involuntary[2] examples of multi-religious and multi-ethnic co-existence have always been the major reason behind the remarkable level of multiculturalism and tolerance existing in Azerbaijan.

Secondly, all state formations and legal systems, established in Azerbaijan in the course of the centuries, have usually sticked to the policy of multiculturalism. Several historical exceptions[3] to this general rule, should not damage a general positive image, as in the majority of cases, they were directed towards the goal of protection of the established beliefs.

Thirdly, current multi-religiosity has a two-fold impact on the religious economy of modern Azerbaijani society: *first of all*, the society has developed an admirably tolerant model and best practices of multiculturalism; *moreover*, it is not always an easy task to maintain the achieved *status quo* due to the phenomena of *"exported religious extremism"*.

Fourthly, Azerbaijan is a comparatively young independent state and its national security has become a target of a number of direct threats and crime. The National Security Concept[4] (2007) of AR encompasses a non-exhaustive list of those threats.

---

[1] Please see the paragraphs 5 and 6 of the speech of the President of Azerbaijan Republic delivered at the opening ceremony of the Third Baku International Humanitarian Forum held on 31 October – 1 November, 2013. The full text is available at: http://en.president.az/articles/9894

[2] *Barbara A. West, Encyclopaedia of the Peoples of Asia and Oceania, pp. 147-149 (2009)*

[3] The movement of Al-Muganna, and Khurremiyya movement. Please see: *M.S. Asimov, C.E. Bosworth, History of Civilisations of Central Asia, Volume IV, p. 46-51 (1999)*. Another example may be the establishment of Shi'ism in Safavids State. Please see: *Elton L. Daniel, The Greenwood Histories of the Modern Nations: The History of Iran, p. 87 (2001)*

[4] *http://www.un.int/azerbaijan/userfiles/file/National_security.pdf)*

Fifthly, although it may seem repetitious, one should mention that regional and global geopolitical dynamics do also play here their role[1].

To summarise, I would like to draw a line between the positive and negative factors mentioned above. So, the long history of multiculturalism (factor 1), well-established state practices of protecting multiculturalism (factor 2), and high levels of interreligious/interethnic tolerance within the civil society (factor 3) can be considered as the positive factors, whereas the last two interconnected and interrelated factors Nos. 4 and 5, balancing national security interests of the state and surviving 'geopolitical waves', are factors which have negative impacts on the FORB in Azerbaijan.

Public and private aspects of FoRB

The latest acts of international terrorism prove the fact that all above-mentioned factors are not the only challenges of modernity. Unfortunately, FoRB itself may also be regarded as a unique and specific factor of threat under current circumstances. On the one hand, international community continue viewing certain suppressive measures taken by subsequent governments as anti-democratic and illegal. On the other hand, the practice proves the fact that sometimes FoRB may culminate in the emergence of territories being disobedient to the secular jurisdictions. Leaving terrorists to benefit from FoRB may thus lead to tragedies, domestic and international chaos. In other words, the most important practical difficulty here is in finding the 'golden ratio' between private and public aspects of FoRB.

This case may also be viewed as one of those cases in which a state faces with practical difficulties in finding the 'golden ratio' between private and public aspects of FoRB. The problem is that various religious manifestations seriously challenge secularism in Azerbaijan. For instance, according to high level State

---

[1] *Tracey German, Regional Cooperation in the South Caucasus: Good Neighbours or Distant Relatives? Chapters 4, 5, 6 and 7, (2012)*

officials, a steady shift is being observed between the quality and quantity of religiosity among young women in Azerbaijan of early 90s and Azerbaijan of today, which derive from *"intra-family atmosphere"*.[1] Azerbaijani authorities, in particular former President and National Leader of Azerbaijan, His Majesty Haydar Aliyev predicted this many years ago and recommended the leadership of the Islamic community "to introduce scientific spirit into Islam".[2]

Thus, the Azerbaijani courts, while deciding the Ijtimai Ittihad Case, did their best to maintain a necessary balance between public and private aspects of FoRB, or secularism and religiosity. Because Azerbaijan is a country where, as the President of AR His Majesty Ilham Aliyev outlines, **"The representatives of all peoples, all the faiths and religions live and will live as one family"**.[3] Any formulas, ideas, principles taking the Azerbaijani society back to the past must be excluded by the law.

Conclusions

Apparently, the findings of the Court in items 3, 4 and 5 above, in particular the urgency and necessity of striking balance between public and private aspects of FoRB, played a decisive role in the final outcome of the trials. The Court applied the principle of proportionality more intensely than the doctrine of *"margin of appreciation"*. Consequently, *"The more intense the standard of proportionality becomes, the narrower the margin allowed to national authorities"*[4].

Nevertheless, the Court, while rightly defending the freedom of association, might leave several questions open which are humbly stipulated below:

---

[1] *Speech of the Head of the Presidential Administration and Academician Mr. Ramiz Mehdiyev on 27 October 2014 during his meeting with the scientific council of the Academy of Public Administration (http://azeridaily.com/politics/1935)*

[2] *"President Ilham Aliyev receives Sheikh ul-Islam Haji Allahshuku Pashazade and a group of religious figures", See § 4 of the press release on the link below:*
(http://azertag.az/en/xeber/PRESIDENT_ILHAM_ALIYEV_RECEIVES_SHEIKH_UL_ISLAM_HAJJI_ALLAHSHUKUR_PASHAZADE_AND_A_GROUP_OF_RELIGIOUS_FIGURES-558820)

[3] http://en.apa.az/xeber_japan_says_close_to_deal_with_south_kore_221000.html

[4] *Yutaka Arai-Takahashi, p. 14*

1. Was the subject-matter of the Case a mere, legal "freedom of association conflict" between the Parties, or was it complicated with other significant elements?
2. Can a juridical person comprising of totally religious members be allowed to get engaged in the activities which are, at least, extremely unpredictable?
3. What are the limits of the *"religiously motivated freedom of association"* within secular societies?

Moreover, the last sentence of § 36 in the Judgment states that, *"The Government submitted that the interference pursued the legitimate aims of "protection of public safety", "protection of the rights and freedoms of others" and "prevention of crimes"*[1]. These seem to be very serious arguments deserving due and thorough contemplations.

I'd like to share further observations which might, at least informally validate the dissolution of the Association. *First of all*, Azerbaijani administration at all levels has centuries-old practices in the adequate and equal treatment of various religious communities. The Government would hardly take any unfair and unnecessary actions against the Association without valid reasons. *Secondly*, Azerbaijani society, like any open and receptive community, is remarkably secular, but also very fragile to religious extremism. *And, last but not least*, Azerbaijan is a part of the global world. The country has no room for religions with political agendas.

---

[1] *http://hudoc.echr.coe.int/sites/eng/pages/search.aspx?i=001-147866#{"itemid":["001-147866"]}*

Bibliography

Literature/Articles

1/ Howard Charles Yourow, The Margin of Appreciation Doctrine in the Dynamics of European Human Rights Jurisprudence, Dordrecht, The Netherlands 1996
2/ Yutaka Arai-Takahashi, The Margin of Appreciation Doctrine and the Principle of Proportionality in the Jurisprudence of ECHR, Oxford 2001
3/ Bernadette Rainey, Concentrate Human Rights Law, Second Edition, Oxford University Press, 2013
4/ Radical Islam in the Former Soviet Union, edited by Galina Yemelianova, New York, 2010
5/ Non-Muslim Minorities in Azerbaijan: from their first inception through Russian Empire and Soviet Repression to present-day Secular State of Azerbaijan, by Willy Fautré, October 2013.
6/ Tracey German, "Regional Cooperation in the South Caucasus: Good Neighbours or Distant Relatives?", Burlington, USA, 2012
7/ Allowing the Right Margin the European Court of Human Rights and the National Margin of Appreciation Doctrine: Waiver or Subsidiarity of European Review"?- by Judge Dean Spielmann, CELS, 2012
8/ "Subsidiarity as a Structural Principle of International Human Rights Law", by Paolo G. Carozza, The American Journal of International Law, Vol.97, No.1 (Jan., 2003), pp.38-79.
9/ "Proportionality and the European Convention on Human Rights" by Jeremy McBride in: The Principle of Proportionality in the Laws of Europe, edited by Evelin Ellis, Oxford, 1999, pp.23-37
10/ "Toward a General Margin of Appreciation Doctrine in International Law", by Yuval Shany, The European Journal of International Law, Vol. 16, No.5, 2006
11/ "Allowing the Right Margin the European Court of Human Rights and the National Margin of Appreciation Doctrine: Waiver or Subsidiarity of European Review"?- by Judge Dean Spielmann, CELS, 2012
12/ *Encyclopaedia of the Peoples of Asia and Oceania,* by Barbara A. West, PH. D., New York, 2009, pp. 147-149.
13/ *History of Civilisations of Central Asia,* Volume IV, by M.S. Asimov and C.E. Bosworth, Delhi, 1999, p. 46-51).
14/ Elton L. Daniel, *The Greenwood Histories of the Modern Nations, The History of Iran,* printed in the USA, 2001 p. 87.

InternationalConventions/Domestic Legislative Acts

1/ ECHR (1950)
2/ Constitution of AR (1995)
3/ Civil Code of AR (2000)
4/ Law on Freedom of Religion (1992)
5/ Law on Non-Governmental Organisations (2000)

Websites

http://hudoc.echr.coe.int/sites/eng/pages/search.aspx?i=001-147866#{"itemid":["001-147866"]}
http://e-qanun.az/files/framework/data/7/f_7649.htm
http://www.venice.coe.int/webforms/documents/default.aspx?pdffile=CDL-REF%282011%29049-e
http://en.wikipedia.org/wiki/Think_globally,_act_locally
https://www.academia.edu/5201189/Non-Muslim_Minorities_in_Azerbaijan_a_Secular_State
www.coe.int/t/dghl/cooperation/lisbonnetwork/Themis/ECHR/Paper2_en.asp#P65_400

http://crrc-caucasus.blogspot.be/2009/02/gallup-azerbaijan-is-one-of-least.html
www.azerbaijans.com/content_617_en.html;
www.jewishvirtuallibrary.org/jsource/vjw/Azerbaijan.html;
http://www.azerbaijan.az/portal/General/Religion/traditionReligion_01_e.html;
http://www.azerbaijan.az/portal/General/Religion/traditionReligion_01_e.html;
http://www.khazaria.com/;
http://lcweb2.loc.gov/cgi-bin/query/r?frd/cstdy:@field(DOCID+az0014 etc.
http://www.un.int/azerbaijan/userfiles/file/National_security.pdf
http://hudoc.echr.coe.int/sites/eng/pages/search.aspx?i=001-147866#{"itemid":["001-147866"]}
http://azeridaily.com/politics/1935
http://azertag.az/en/xeber/PRESIDENT_ILHAM_ALIYEV_RECEIVES_SHEIKH_UL_ISLAM_HAJJI_ALLAHSHUKUR_PASHAZADE_AND_A_GROUP_OF_RELIGIOUS_FIGURES-558820

www.coe.int/t/dlapil/codexter/Source/country_profiles/CODEXTER%20Profiles%20%282007%29%20Azerbaijan%20E.pdf

Cases

1/ *Seyidzade v. Azerbaijan*, no. 37700/05, §§ 31-40, 3 December 2009
2/ *Rasmussen v. Denmark*, No.8777/79, 28 Nov., 1984
3/ *Sunday Times v. United Kingdom*, no.6538/74, 26 Apr. 1979, § 59
4/ *Lautsi and others v. Italy*, no.30814/16, 18 March 2011
5/ *Juma Mosque Congregation and Others v. Azerbaijan*, no.15405/04, 08 Jan. 2013

CHAPTER 2. ARTICLES

Article No 1. Freedom of Religion and Belief in Azerbaijan (FoRB): current legal regime, contemporary challenges and safeguards

Summary

This article has been dedicated to one of the significant problems of out times. It discusses several aspects of the legal FoRB regime in Azerbaijan Republic. First of all, the author takes a look at the historical roots of FoRB very briefly. Then, he provides analysis of the four pillars of the Azerbaijani legal FoRB regime and discusses the appropriate legal principles. Furthermore, he compiles a list of challenges for FoRB in Azerbaijan. He also reviews factors mitigating and or aggravating those challenges.

Keywords: *freedom of religion and belief, the FoRB regime, pillars of the Azerbaijani FoRB regime, constitutional pillar, legislative pillar, restorative pillar, institutional pillar, principles of the Azerbaijani FoRB regime, challenges for the Azerbaijani FoRB regime, factors mitigating of aggravating challenges for the Azerbaijani FoRB.*

Introduction

It is worth noting that this article does not pretend to be an exhaustive treatment of all FoRB-related issues throughout the world. It merely intends to provide a brief overview of the legal FoRB regime in Azerbaijan Republic. However, it seems fit-for-purpose to start with a very short passage on the roots of the FoRB phenomenon.

FoRB is a relatively new legal concept, which is designed to embrace a wide range of complex and challenging realities in the religious domain in the current turbulent environments. Obviously, it has numerous ancestors each of which met the requirements of its time. For example, we may refer to Syncretism [1, 1-25] as a dominant ideology within the community of traders or the Muslim tradition of dhimmis [2, 50, § 2]. Appropriate provisions of numerous legal instruments including but not limited to the Cyrus Cylinder, the Edicts of Ashoka, the Edict of Torda, Virginia Statute for Religious Freedom etc. did also provide a certain level of legal protection for the religious freedom.

In modern ages, the constitutions and other legislative acts of almost all countries contain appropriate provisions regarding the equivalent protection of the freedom of religion [3, 191-559]. What about international law, one of the first and most significant legal instruments with global effect was the 1948 Universal Declaration of Human Rights, which recognised everyone's right to freedom of thought, conscience and religion in its Article 18. The 1981 Declaration on the Elimination of all Forms of Intolerance and of Discrimination Based on Religion or Belief is another international legal document with its three potentially far-reaching non-discrimination provisions [4, 42-43].

I. The legal FoRB regime in Azerbaijan Republic

Getting back on FoRB in Azerbaijan, I find it appropriate to underline two important issues. *First of all*, despite the fact that Azerbaijan stands today shoulder to shoulder with the civil law countries and its legal system is based on civil law, in my humble opinion, this country can be considered as a part of a unique legal geography where material sources of law usually prevailed formal sources throughout the centuries until the XX century. In particular, material legal sources, which emerged thanks to the influential and widely respected representatives of various religions, including Zoroastrianism, Tengrism, Judaism, Christianity and Islam played an exclusive role in decision-making and socio-political life of the country in general [5, 60].

As history witnesses, this approach to law, society and state proved to be highly effective in Azerbaijan, thus contributing to the evolution of reliable governing practices and multicultural environments. Otherwise, it would be extremely difficult and almost impossible to cope with the challenges and threats of our times. Because there are a number of factors continuously affecting FORB environments in Azerbaijan [6, 5-6]. They will be discussed in the last two sections of this article.

Thanks to effective governing practices, contemporary Azerbaijani society is highly tolerant and friendly towards the representatives of all other cultures, despite the country's extremely sensitive geographical location, which makes Azerbaijan to face with a wide range of trans-border challenges, such as separatism, terrorism, regional conflicts etc. [7, 5, Articles 3.2 to 3-11], including attempts against the independence, sovereignty, territorial integrity, and constitutional order of the Republic of Azerbaijan [7, 5, Article 3.1].

Undoubtedly, it would be extremely difficult to manage those challenges without appropriate legal tools. The country possesses a valid and effective legal regime, which helps it in dealing with them. The national legal FoRB regime in Azerbaijan is constructed on the following **four separate pillars**:

1. *Constitutional pillar.* This pillar is the foundation of the legal hierarchy and pyramid, which sets forth the fundamental legal norms and principles related to the freedom of religion and belief in the most important legal instrument of the country. It is based upon the appropriate constitutional provisions [8, the last item in the Preamble and the provisions in the Article 18 of the Constitution] and can be divided into two sub-categories. The first sub-category consists of several principles. I would prefer to start the discussion of the constitutional pillar with a declarative statement in the Preamble of the Constitution. It includes in the list of the constitutionally declared aims of the Azerbaijani people: *"to remain faithful to universal values, to live in friendship, peace and*

security with all the nations of the world, and to cooperate with them for this purpose". Thus, I may humbly admit that **humanism** is the very first fundamental principle of the constitutional pillar.

Furthermore, the Constitution of Azerbaijan Republic separates religion from the state while making all religions equal before the law. Thus, we may conclude that **secularism** constitutes the second principle of the constitutional pillar of the Azerbaijani FoRB. As it becomes obvious from the above postulate, secularism is followed by the principle of inter-religious **equality**. The next principle is *'tolerated' (or 'required') restriction*, which allows the state authorities to prevent the dissemination of the inhuman and degrading religious ideologies. This principle does also require that the education system must be based upon the principle of secularism, which makes Azerbaijan one of few among the members of the Council of Europe that has a direct legal constitutional reference to the secularity of public education [9, 42].

If the first subcategory of the constitutional pillar concentrates on the regulation of **state-religion relationships** in general, then its second subcategory aims at dealing with **the human-religion-state triangle** [8, Article 48 of the Constitution]. Therefore, the very first principle under the second subcategory is the principle of human **freedom** in determining his approach to religion. This kind of freedom encompasses the right to be free from being forced to get involved, by words or by deeds, a part of any religion.

However, here again, the state enjoys a set of exclusive legal opportunities designed to protect three fundamental values: *a) public interests; b) morality; c) and the law*. The realisation of any religious right that disturbs public order, is contrary to public morals, or violates the law will not be constitutionally tolerated on the territories of Azerbaijan Republic. Thus, we may just discover the second principle of the second subcategory of the constitutional pillar, which is the principle of **protection**.

Finally, the third principle under the second subcategory is *privacy* stipulating that it can never be allowed to force someone to proclaim his religion, thoughts and belief [8, Article 71].

2. *Legislative pillar.* Obviously, legislation is a continuous process and it is therefore a little bit more effective and flexible pillar of FoRB in any country. The reason is that the contemporary FoRB-related issues are highly dynamic and changing phenomena, which requires instant and case-by-case reaction in order to deal with its challenges properly. From this perspective, the legislative pillar creates a more practical legal regime capable of coping with a wide range of FoRB-related problems.

The importance of the legislation is also in the fact that its separate instruments (in particular, laws) contain numerous legal provisions detailing the constitutional principles on FoRB, identifying the scope and limits of their application, eliminating the gaps, and dealing with a number of other issues of practical-legal importance.

The legislative pillar of the legal Azerbaijani FoRB regime is based upon several laws and other legislative acts, the most important of which is 'the Freedom of Religious Belief' Act [10]. On the basis of Article 1 of the mentioned Law, we may take into consideration the following legislative standards applied within the FoRB regime in Azerbaijan:

- The constitutional religious freedom can be realised individually or collectively;
- Forcible propaganda of religion is prohibited;
- Dissemination of religious ideas is strictly linked to the 'nationality' principle;
- The law recognises the right of parents to educate their children in accordance with their religious belief.

3. ***Restorative pillar.*** This pillar is usually considered as the last level of protection of the legal FoRB regime. It consists of appropriate legal norms and standards too. However, this pillar is organised of 'post factum' norms and rules. They start operating from the moment of violation of the principles and norms, which form the previous two (constitutional or legislative) pillars. Their major task is to restore the pre-violation status quo to the maximum extent possible or recover damages and sufferings. Consequently, restorative norms possess a different structure than the norms forming previous pillars. As a rule, it is quite possible to locate not only hypothesis and disposition, but also a sanction – coercive element [11, 50-51] in the structure of the restorative norms. The sanction part of the norm does also define all possible variants of necessary legal action to be taken by the proper governmental authority. In my humble opinion, we may consider the following subcategories of the restorative pillar:

    *a) **Administrative legal pillar.*** Administrative norms and standards are rules of general applicability, which both facilitate or constrain the realisation of administrative policy objectives of the government [11, 49]. In principal, those norms and standards can be found in a huge single legal instrument, usually called a code [13]. The Azerbaijani administrative legal pillar declares unlawful the following actions:
- *violation of order of establishment and activity of religious structures may lead to the imposition of penalty in amount of 10-15 manats (on natural persons) and of 40-70 manats (on official persons) [13, Article 299];*
- *spreading the religious ideologies in violation of the 'nationality' principle (may lead to the deportation or imposition of money penalty in amount of 20-25 manats) etc [13, Article 300].*

    *b) **Criminal legal pillar.*** Apparently, this sub-pillar is not less important than the administrative legal pillar. It also consists of a set of solid legal norms and standards, which start operating as soon as the FoRB regime, established by the first (foundation pillar) and second (medium pillar) pillars, fail to operate properly. Thus, criminal legal pillar may be described as the top of the legal hierarchy and pyramid designed to protect the legal FoRB regime in Azerbaijan Republic.

Of course, there is an essential difference between the two sub-pillars of the restorative pillar. The mentioned difference is very closely linked with the differences between 'administrative violations' and 'crimes'. Obviously, all offences are socially dangerous, illegal, guilty and punishable. However, the signs like object, nature and degree of social danger, nature of illegality, and nature of results allow to differ the crime from other offences [14, 44-45].

The major legal instrument forming the criminal legal pillar in Azerbaijan is Criminal Code of Azerbaijan Republic. According to its provisions, the perpetration of any crime on the grounds of national, racial or religious hatred is one of the circumstances aggravating punishment *[15, Article 61.1.6]*. Furthermore, the Code criminalises the act of genocide *[15, Article 103]*, discrimination [15, Article 109], violation of laws and customs of war [15, Article 115], deliberate murder on motives of national, racial, religious hatred or enmity [115, Article 120.2.12], impending implementation of religious activities [115, Article 167], forcing others to embrace any religion [115, Article 167-1], producing or publishing, importing, selling or distributing religious literature, things or other informative materials illegally [115, Article 167-2], encroaching on the rights of others under the pretext of implementation of religious rituals [115, Article 168], and causing hatred and enmity on national, racial, social or religious grounds [115, Article 283].

II. Institutional safeguards for FoRB in Azerbaijan

I did not cover *the fourth pillar* of the Azerbaijani legal FoRB regime in the previous section, as it possesses several distinctive features. *First of all,* the elements constituting the fourth pillar may be considered as the material sources of law, as they hold enormous practical opportunities to give birth, directly or indirectly, to new legal standards and rules. *Secondly,* they are 'alive' organisms acting on behalf of the state. *Thirdly,* the mentioned elements must always act in accordance with the requirements of the first, second and third pillars. They have no autonomy to violate already existing norms of law.

Briefly speaking, the fourth pillar encompasses appropriate public and private agencies operating to ensure the well-being of the national FoRB regime in Azerbaijan. We may put those institutions into appropriate categories, including public and private agencies, executive, legislative and judicial agencies, secular and religious institutions, governmental and non-governmental institutions etc. However, I would like to focus on the following institutional safeguards for the purposes of this article.

The Milli Majlis of Azerbaijan Republic is a key legislative body, which takes an active part in the creation and improvement of the first, second and third pillars. The Milli Majlis adopts constitutional laws, laws and resolutions concerning issues falling under its competence [8, Article 93.1]. The Milli Majlis has updated the Azerbaijani Law on the Freedom of Religious Belief 76 times [10] since its adoption in 1992.

The President of Azerbaijan Republic is the central figure not only for the improvement of the first, second and third pillars, but also for the operation of the many state agencies included in the fourth pillar. The President signs laws, constitutional laws [8, Article 110], issues decrees and orders [8, Article 113]. Besides that, Article 96 of the Constitution enables the President of Azerbaijan Republic to submit draft laws and other questions for the consideration of the Milli

Majlis (the right to legislative initiative). Assistant to the President of Azerbaijan Republic for Multinational Relations, Multiculturalism, and Religious Issues fulfils important tasks by preparing appropriate reports, providing expertise, holding meetings etc.

The State Committee for Work with Religious Organisations is in charge of regulation of activities of religious organisations and ensuring freedom of religion in Azerbaijan. The Committee is a kind of bridge between the secular state system and religious communities in the country. Thus, one should not underestimate the Committee's role, as it is a central executive body responsible for the formation of the governmental policies in the given domain [16]. The Committee works in close cooperation with a number of religious organisations, which represent their subsequent religions, including the Spiritual Board of Caucasian Muslims, the Russian Orthodox Church, the Jewish Community, the Catholic Church and many others.

Finally, it is necessary to mention the Azerbaijani law enforcement agencies successfully operating in the sphere of combatting religious extremism and radical religious ideologies. Different ministries, committees and services (Ministry of Internal Affairs, Ministry of Justice etc.) of Azerbaijan Republic join together to reveal and prevent religiously motivated acts of violation in a timely manner. Azerbaijani courts are also active guards of the third – restorative pillar widely discussed in the previous section.

Thus, the number 4 is a central, crucial and operative pillar in dealing with numerous challenges directed against the FoRB regime in Azerbaijan.

III. Challenges for FoRB

The vast majority of those challenges are of the political, military, even geopolitical etc. character. Therefore, a detailed discussion of such elements in an article dedicated to the legal aspects of the freedom of religion does not seem fit-for-purpose. In this section, I find it appropriate to provide a short list of challenges threatening the national legal FoRB regime in Azerbaijan Republic, which includes but is not limited to the following:

- Unresolved/frozen Conflicts;
- Politically motivated radical separatism;
- Religiously motivated radical ideologies;
- Religious Extremism;
- Terrorism;
- Transnational Organized Crime.

Furthermore, I would like to draw a line between the positive and negative factors mitigating or aggravating the above challenges. So, the long history of multiculturalism (factor 1), well-established state practices of respecting multiculturalism (factor 2), and high levels of interreligious/interethnic tolerance within the civil society (factor 3) can be considered as the positive factors, whereas the last two interconnected and interrelated factors Nos. 4 and 5 - balancing national security interests of the state and surviving 'geopolitical waves' are factors which may have negative impacts on the legal FoRB regime in Azerbaijan Republic.

Conclusions

In the current section, the previously enumerated 'mitigating' or 'aggravating' factors are to be detailed in the light of the previous section on challenges. *First of all*, the history of the progress of the Azerbaijani religious economy needs to be taken into account. This country has been a land of clashes and dialogues between/among several religions, particularly, various practices of heathenism (animism, shamanism etc.) and Zoroastrianism, Judaism, Christianity, Islam, 'Imposed Atheism' and finally Secularism throughout centuries until recently [17] [18]. In my humble opinion, this centuries-old and persistent, even though sometimes involuntary, example of multi-religious (and multi-ethnic) co-existence has always been the major reason behind the remarkable level of multiculturalism and tolerance existing in Azerbaijan. The history of Caucasus Albania is an important proof of the hard and non-stable religious practices in the nowadays territories of the Republic of Azerbaijan due to its geographical location [19, 147-149].

Secondly, all state formations and political, religious and legal systems, once established in Azerbaijan in the course of centuries, have usually sticked to the policy of multiculturalism and done their best to preserve and respect the multicultural environments and tolerance atmosphere in the lands under their jurisdiction due to objective reasons (particularly, the need for peace, widely spread inter-religious and inter-ethnic royal/noble marriages etc.). And, of course, several exceptions [20, 46-51] [21, 87] to this general rule, which took part in the past, should not damage a generally positive image, as in the majority of cases, they were directed towards the goal of protection of the established beliefs. At this point, it seems highly fit-for-purpose to quote the national leader of Azerbaijan Republic His Excellency Haydar Aliyev who once said in 1996: "Historically, world religions have co-existed and respected each other in Azerbaijan. The Azerbaijani state is still loyal to its traditions. Freedom of conscience and freedom of faith are the spiritual wealth of our society" [22].

Thirdly, current multi-religiosity has a two-fold impact on the religious economy of modern Azerbaijan society: *first of all*, the government and society has developed an admirably tolerant model and best practices of multiculturalism; *moreover*, it is not always an easy task to maintain the achieved *status quo* in the sphere of the FoRB due to the phenomena of ***exported religious extremism***.

Fourthly, Azerbaijan is a comparatively young independent state and its national security has become a target of a number of direct threats and crime and the National Security Concept (2007) of the Republic of Azerbaijan encompasses a non-exhaustive list of those threats [7].

Fifthly, although it may seem repetitious, one should mention that regional and global geopolitical dynamics do also play here their role [23, chapters 4, 5, 6 and 7].

Finally, the existence of numerous non-legal challenges is not considered as an obstacle for the realisation of the highest objective of the Azerbaijani state. Under Article 12 of the Azerbaijani Constitution, the state ensures rights and freedoms of man and citizen, and a proper standard of living to the citizens. Moreover, the rights and freedoms, including religious rights enumerated in the Constitution are applied in accordance with not only the domestic legislation, but also the norms of international law contained in international treaties to which Azerbaijan Republic is a party.

Used literature

1. Syncretism / Anti – syncretism: the politics of religious synthesis, edited by Charles Stewart and Rosalind Shaw, published by Routledge, London and New York, 2005.
2. Bat Ye'or, Islam and Dhimmitude: where civilisations collide, translated from the French by Miriam Kochan and David Littman, printed in the United States of America, 2002.
3. Religious Human Rights in Global Perspective: Legal Aspects, edited by Johan D. Van Der Vyver and John Witte, Jr., printed in the Netherlands, Kluwer Law International, 1996.
4. Julian Rivers, The Law of Organised Religions: Between Establishment and Secularism, Oxford University Press, 2010.
5. Ismail bey Zerdabli, The History of Azerbaijan: from ancient times to the present day, published by Rossendale Books, London, 2014.
6. Ramin Aliyev, Case of Islam-Ittihad Association v. Azerbaijan, an essay submitted to the Faculty of Canon Law at KU Leuven, 2015. The full text of the essay is available on the following link: https://www.academia.edu/10617155/Essay_on_the_Ijtimai_Ittihad_v._Azerbaijan_Case
7. National Security Concept of the Azerbaijan Republic, Approved by Instruction No. 2198 of the President of the Republic of Azerbaijan on 3 May 2007.
8. The Constitution of Azerbaijan Republic, 1995.
9. Handbook of Religious Education, edited by Derek H. Davis and Elena Miroshnikova, published the Routledge International, New York, 2013.
10. The Law of the Republic of Azerbaijan on Freedom of Religious Belief, 1992.
11. Hans Kelsen, General Theory of Law and State, translated by Anders Wedberg, the Lawbook Exchange, LTD. Clark, New Jersey, 2007.
12. Peter Cane, Administrative Law, Clarendon Law Series, Oxford University Press, Fifth Edition, 2011.
13. The Code of Azerbaijan Republic on Administrative Violations, 2000.
14. Isfandiyar Aghayev, Criminal Law (The General Part), Leipziger Universitatsverlag GMBH, 2015.
15. Criminal Code of Azerbaijan Republic, 2000.
16. http://www.azerbaijan.az/portal/StatePower/Committee/committeeConcern_02_e.html
17. http://www.azerbaijan.az/portal/General/Religion/traditionReligion_01_e.html

18. http://www.jewishvirtuallibrary.org/azerbaijan-virtual-jewish-history-tour
19. Encyclopaedia of the Peoples of Asia and Oceania, by Barbara A. West, PH. D., New York, 2009.
20. History of Civilisations of Central Asia, Volume IV, by M.S. Asimov and C.E. Bosworth, Delhi, 1999.
21. Elton L. Daniel, the Greenwood Histories of the Modern Nations, The History of Iran, printed in the USA, 2001.
22. From the congratulation of Orthodox Christians of the republic on the occasion of Easter - April 15, 1996. The Internet source: http://multiculturalism.preslib.az/en_testimonials-ha.html
23. Tracey German, "Regional Cooperation in the South Caucasus: Good Neighbours or Distant Relatives?" Published by Ashgate Publishing Limited, Burlington, USA, 2012.

Article No 2. Apocalypses already knock at our doors: two 'invisible' chances for surviving...

Keywords: *Armed conflicts; separatism; terrorism; International Law; United Nations.*

Introduction

The modern global system eroded old boundaries between foreign and domestic affairs. The global century now requires governments everywhere to see, think, and act globally. Where democratic and adaptive governments are in place, globalization is fostering stability and prosperity. But the widening gap between many countries with weak or authoritarian governments and the rest of the world feeds instability at all levels.

Thus the 'major evils' of modern ages consist of the so-called 'giant global networks' (GGNs) which operates in many countries and include in: a) antidemocratic governments; b) imperialistic power centers; c) a set of transnational corporations; d) several intergovernmental organizations; e) groups involved in transnational organized crime. Unfortunately, such networks sometimes are apologized and incited, or even supported by the democratic governments and organizations for their own political, economic, financial, geostrategic, military etc. interests.

The latter sensitive case results in the increase of 'interminable' negative impacts and consequences of globalization, which can be divided into two broad categories: *First,* the image of democracy and global democratic forces are extensively damaged and antidemocratic authorities in the world get stronger day by day; *Second,* all elements of the 'major evil' remain unprosecuted and unpunished, despite the fact that they altogether commit a number of internationally recognized crimes, and their ideologists insist on the 'necessity' and 'legitimacy' of such illegal acts saying that 'their perpetration were necessary as if for sake of the country's, people's safety, or national security etc. The resulting economic and social disparities intensify and aggravate inter-communal grievances, religious and ethnic tensions, generate terrorism and armed conflicts.

All of the above-mentioned places new and urgent demands on global democratic forces. Transnational risks are growing every next day, which threaten the future of the humankind with the possibility of the misuse of nuclear weapons as well. In other words, apocalypses already knock at our doors…

We have one and 'invisible' chance for surviving. It is the international law which should bind the members of the international community to specific values, standards and norms of behavior. Of course, thanks to our ancestors, **Permissive International Law** (PIL) developed at the necessary scale. The only thing that we have to do is to promote and put into practice the norms of **Coercive International Law** (CIL), in order to increase its effectiveness.

Globally discussed, agreed, forced and implemented legal norms need a necessary global platform to create them. We have it under our hands at the moment. Even if some observers question whether the U.N. can foster peace and stability and even if we do not see it…

Just imagine for a moment that the U.N., its charter and the current global security system does not exist!

And the existence of the crisis within the U.N. system is another question to be dealt with. Addressing this challenge requires: **First,** we have to SEE the U.N at least; **Second**, we need to improve the U.N. system in order to make it stronger, more effective and more elastic to meet growing global security interests.

Paying the price: 'crying' figures

Many international state-related and/or non-governmental scientific organizations carry out multidisciplinary researches directed towards the goals of elaborating a comprehensive definition, identifying the root causes and becoming aware of the suffered human losses and damages of politically motivated domestic and transnational violence. For example, the Uppsala Conflict Data Program (UCDP) defines [1] conflict as: "a contested incompatibility that concerns government and/or territory where the use of armed force between two parties, of which at least one is the government of a state, results in at least 25 battle-related deaths." According to the UCDP several separate elements of the definition are to be distinguished, including the 'use of armed force', 'arms', '25 deaths'.

A document compiled by Monty G. Marshall, the Center for Systemic Peace Director and titled 'Major Episodes of Political Violence [2] lists **315 episodes of armed conflict**(including **26 ongoing cases**) in the world over the contemporary period: 1946-2009. "Major episodes of political violence" involve at least 500 "directly-related" fatalities and reach a level of intensity in which political violence is both systematic and sustained (a base rate of 100 "directly-related deaths per annum"). Episodes may be of any general type: inter-state, intra-state, or communal; they include all episodes of international, civil, ethnic, communal, and genocidal violence and warfare.

The activists of the Canadian "Project Ploughshares" documented 40 conflicts in 2000. By the end of 2008 they recorded 28 conflicts being fought in 24 countries. Despite the fact that 2008 saw a return to prevailing downward trend in armed conflicts, majority of the contemporary armed conflicts are accompanied by the intermittent fighting and involves many levels of dangerous intensity. And the "Ploughshares" compiled the following table indicating geographic distribution of armed conflicts in 2008 [3]:

Region	# of countries in region	# of conflicts in region	# of countries hosting conflicts	% of countries in region hosting conflicts	% of world conflicts

Africa	50	11	10	20	39.3
Asia	42	11	8	19	39.3
Europe	42	1	1	2.4	3.6
The Americas	44	1	1	2	3.6
Middle East	14	4	4	29	14.2
World Totals	*192*	*28*	*24*	*12.5*	*100*

According to UNICEF, in the last decades child victims of armed conflict include 2 million children killed, 4-5 million children disabled, 2 million children left homeless, more than 1 million children orphaned or separated from their parents, some 10 million children traumatized. This means that, on average, more than 2,000 children are being killed, maimed or disabled by war every single day [4].

Year by year the situation is going from bad to worse. The researches and records of the international NGOs demonstrate that, only between 1945 and 1992 there were 149 major wars, killing more than 23 million people. This figure is considered to be more than double the deaths of the 19th century and seven times greater than 18th century. More disastrously, 90 % of war victims were noncombatants and at least half of these were children. Since the end of the cold war, there have been 57 major armed conflicts. There has been observed a steady decline in the number of conflicts since 1999, and the figure for 2005 is the lowest for the entire post-cold war period (17 major armed conflicts in 16 locations).

However the post-communist era brought a new wave of political violence-rooted and in particular, conflict-caused human causalities deriving from the collapse of the former USSR and Yugoslavia, and interstate wars in Balkans, Afghanistan and Iraq, and intertribal fighting in Rwanda, Cambodia etc. The former USSR political crisis indicating figures make the international society informed about the extremely dangerous future perspectives of this region alone. A number of coup d'état attempts in Russia, Georgia, Azerbaijan, the Georgian civil war (1991-1993), the Tajikistani civil war (1992-1997), ongoing separatist conflicts in Chechnya (Russian Federation), Transnistria (Moldova), Abkhazia and South Ossetia (Georgia), Nagorno Garabakh (Azerbaijan), Russian-Georgia war (2008) etc. destabilized the local societies, damaged national economies and infrastructures, thus resulted in catastrophic human causalities and sufferings. In Balkans one should remember also War in Slovenia (1991), Croatian War of Independence (1991-1995), Bosnian War (1992-1995), and Kosovo War (1998-1999). Only "Yugoslavian Dissolution Wars" (1991-1995) took lives of more than 20,000 Croats, 64,000 Bosnians and Herzegovinians, 36,000 Serbs.

The UN Assistance Mission in Afghanistan (UNAMA) reported that 2,118 Afghan civilians were killed by armed conflict in 2008, the highest number since the end of the initial 2001 invasion. This represented an increase of about 40% over UNAMA's figure of 1,523 Afghan civilians killed in 2007 [5]. 'Opinion Research Business Survey' reports that since March 2003 more than 1,000,000 violent deaths occurred as a result of the conflict in Iraq. According to a Human Rights estimate, at least 800,000 people were killed in 1994 in Rwanda [6].

Another disastrous and almost the "oldest" armed confrontation of modern ages is Israeli-Palestinian conflict which started in the late 19th century. Founded in 1989, B'Tselem or "The Israeli Information Center for Human Rights in the Occupied Territories" may be seen as one of the Israeli protective organizations documenting human rights violations in the Occupied Territories, contributing to the work of creation of human right culture in the country and educating Israeli public about human rights problems. Between 1987-2000, 1545 Palestinians and 421 Israelis, from 2000 until 2004 3194 Palestinians and 946 Israelis, and since 2005 more than 3230 Palestinians and 133 Israelis lost their lives, according to the "B'Tselem" causality figures.

Other sources claim "the First Intifada [7]" years in Palestine (1987-1993) took the lives of 2,162 Palestinians and 164 Israelis. Consequently, the "Second Intifada" or "the Al-Aqsa Intifada" period (2000-2008) killed at least 5,500 Palestinians and 1,062 Israelis. One should also speak about the "Gaza War" which took place in the Gaza Strip and was codenamed "Mivtza Oferet Yetzuka" [8]. 1,417 Palestinians and 13 Israelis killed, 5,303 Palestinians and 518 Israelis were wounded as the result of the mentioned war. Most recently Israel Defense Forces realized another military operation code named the "Operation See Breeze" taking the lives of several human rights activists and thus generating an undesirable diplomatic scandal between Ankara and Tel-Aviv.

Unfortunately, nowadays the world is just watching how hundreds of non-combatant and innocent human beings are victimized in Kyrgyzstan. Several unofficial resources report at least 2,000 ethnic Uzbeks killed since the beginning of inter-ethnic clashes. The mass killings are performed with a specific cruelty – many victims are raped, burned alive etc. This forced two international non-governmental organizations to take at least some action in order to prevent genocidal acts on the Kyrgyz territories and stabilize the situation to some extent. Ms. Louise Arbour, the 'International Crisis Group' president and CEO and Mr. Kenneth Roth, the 'Human Rights Watch' executive director compiled and announced a joint letter to the United Nations Security Council urging it 'to take immediate steps to address the ongoing crisis in Kyrgyzstan'. Furthermore, the letter points out that 'The threat to regional peace and security posed by the crisis in Kyrgyzstan is real and, despite the reduction in daily violence, still growing'.

Here a particular attention must be concentrated on the most important and most positive aspect of the above-mentioned letter: it recalls on the Security Council's obligation to respond to such kind of risks. Moreover, the authors say 'the Security Council should act immediately to work with the government, regional organizations and others to prevent further escalation of violence, including by authorizing international law enforcement and security assistance' [9]. It means they notice the 'bloody tears' of those figures, and hold a different position in comparison with the thousands of top national politicians, who pursue continuous, systematical and comprehensive strategies and policies directed towards the goal of FUELLING CONFLICT...

FUELLING CONFLICT: Is the UN Security System effective enough to prevent?

The near past's global organizational and legal *"problem-solving system"* and practice completely disappointed the majority of the Globe's citizens. This system's central ring – the UN failed at doing many things falling within the scope of its mandate. So what was the major reason originating the ineffectiveness of the UN system? Are humans inherently so violent? Or the *reptilians from another star system* are the force behind a worldwide conspiracy directed at humanity? May be the peoples of the Globe should consider all those bloody events as steps in an on-going plot to achieve world domination through secret political gatherings and decision-making processes?

May be 50 years ago we could speak about the extremely violent nature of humans. But now we should never forget that all kinds of acts of mass violence take place for one ultimate goal: SURVIVAL! Thus, the international society should pay much more attention to the controlling of *"global resource-oriented confrontations"*, which could be put into following categories:

- Political confrontations over human resources. They take place at international and particularly domestic levels. At national levels they are seen in the majority of antidemocratic regimes (e.g., the "power thirst" rulers and clans);
- Political and economic confrontations over territories (land, water and air, including outer space). They have basically strategic and sometimes mixed purposes;
- Political and/or economic confrontations over the huge energy resources;

- Ideological confrontations directed to the goals of reshaping, reforming and controlling minds, traditions, religious thoughts and rituals of peoples, and "ideological centers", including religious objects as well. These ones serve the goal of manufacturing a "voluntary" consensus of the governed masses. Here we have to reconsider a "propaganda model" that Herman and Chomsky put forward in *Manufacturing Consent* (1988);
- Confrontations and manipulations over food, "physical maintenance" and health resources.

Here one should mention warnings most recently sounded by a distinguished Australian professor of microbiology Mr. Frank Fenner. As many of you may be already aware of the matter, on 19 June 2010 the leading scientist claimed that 'Human race and a lot of other animals will be unable to survive a population explosion and unbridled consumption'. He also said that 'Climate change is just at the very beginning. But we're seeing remarkable changes in the weather already'. Simon Ross, the vice-chairman of the Optimum Population Trust also enumerated mankind's real challenges including climate change, loss of biodiversity and unprecedented growth in population, thus supporting Mr. Fenner's views [10].

The position of the Global Humanitarian Forum [11], which focused its activities on human impact of climate change, is very similar to the above-mentioned views. The major outcome of the Forum's activities, a comprehensive report titled 'Anatomy of silent crises' outlines that 'Climate change is already responsible for 300,000 deaths a year. Economic losses due to climate change amount today $125bn a year. Four billion people are vulnerable now and 500m are at extreme risk. Civil unrest may also increase because of weather-related events, including hunger, disease, poverty and lost livelihoods'. The report additionally projects that severe heat waves, floods, storms, and forest fires will be responsible for as many as 500,000 deaths a year by 2030, and by the same year climate change could cost $600bn a year [12].

Logically, all of the Globe's nations should unite under such heavy circumstances. Unfortunately, top policy-makers and strategists of several world nations believe that their people could survive alone even if the other ones perish and they still strongly adhere to the principle of 'Divide and rule'. Those governments still hold "crisis factories" with the goal of "manufacturing conflicts". And this fact seriously endangers the future of international peace and security and damages the foundations of the global security system. *The so-called 'crisis factories' consist of several 'sections' or 'divisions', which include arms trade, supporting separatist movements, sponsoring terrorism, exporting radical ideologies, suppressing human rights and totally eliminating democracy or giving birth to an 'on-paper democracies', orchestrating ethnic conflicts, civil wars and riots, creating necessary conditions for the proliferation of WMD, granting assistance to the perpetrators of international crimes, aggravating the work of law enforcement agencies in the sphere of combating transnational organized crime etc.*

Undoubtedly, arms trade fuels conflict and leads to an increase in casualties. For example, a Canadian peace-oriented project, 'the Campaign against Arms Trade (CAAT)' works for the reduction and ultimate abolition of the international arms trade, together with progressive demilitarization within arms-producing countries. CAAT believes that 'If we really want to prevent millions of children from being seriously harmed and killed in armed conflict, one of the first things we need to do is to abolish the deadly trade in armaments' [13].

We should also remember another example. *Ze'ev Wolfson **[14]** stated that* 'At the moment when the USSR collapsed, the 7 Guard Army, numbering approximately 23,000 soldiers, was stationed in Armenia. Toward the middle of 1992, two of the Army's three divisions were transferred to Armenian control. The Army's materiel was distributed according to the Tashkent Collective Security Treaty of 1992. The distribution was actually completed by the end of the year. Armenia thus received about 360 tanks, over 100 BMP infantry fighting vehicles of other types, 130 artillery pieces [15].

Azerbaijani media outlets repeatedly report that Russian defense officials transfer weapons and other military hardware worth US$ 800 million to Armenia in 2008. The evidence consisted of a document containing the signature of a Russian defense official and a detailed list of the transferred weapons. As becomes clear from the document, the weapons used to belong to a Russian military bases in Georgia, which was later withdrawn in accordance with OSCE requirements and relocated to Armenia. At that time, Russian political and military officials responded to Azerbaijani concerns about the relocation by stating that the weapons and other military equipment in the military base would remain the property of the Russian Federation, and would not be transferred to Armenia [16].

However, the UN still lacks powerful and effective mechanisms in the field of disarmament. The Charter provisions concerning the disarmament issues simply provide that the General Assembly 'consider general principles of cooperation…including the principles governing disarmament and the regulation of armaments; make recommendations with regard to such principles to the members or the Security Council or to both' (Article 11.1). Surely, no force could prevent such kind of global and 'speedy armament' only by making recommendations. This is the fundamental reason why today's Iranian nuclear crisis can not be solved so far. Even in case of the emergence of real nuclear armament threats several key states hesitate or deliberately 'fail' acting for the effective and timely application of the 1968 Treaty on the Non-Proliferation of Nuclear Weapons.

Supporting separatism is another phenomena fuelling armed violence in modern ages. By definition, 'Separatism is the advocacy of a state of cultural, ethnic, tribal, religious, racial, governmental or gender separation from the larger group, often with demands for greater political autonomy and even for full political secession and the formation of a new state'[17]. In particular, ethnic and religious movements with the separatist political agendas stress the contemporary world by giving birth to 'geopolitical entities', which claim statehood in accordance with the declarative theory of statehood[18]. Abkhazia, South Ossetia,

Transnistria, and Nagorno Karabakh constitute four examples of ethnic separatism supported openly or secretly by one powerful and several other states.

In modern ages separatism is often mixed with the self-determination of peoples. The latter one is a principle contained in the Charter (Article 1.1) and since 1947 it successfully backed the collapse of several colonial emperies and facilitated the promotion of democracy. But now the world must keep itself far from the illusions. The modern global system is undoubtedly obliged to prefer the maintenance of peace and security to self-determination. And globalization processes must be accompanied with the global anti-separatist tendencies. Any researcher can face with an ironic situation, when he or she discovers the contradictory correlation between the current jus cogens norms of international law and state practices in relation to the settlement of disputes and conflicts. For example, the UN Charter postulates that states ought to endeavor to settle their disputes peacefully and never use force (Article 2.3 and 2.4). Thus the use of force is strictly restricted and may arise only in the form of individual or collective self-defense (Article 51). However, the use of force by separatist circles, groups, organizations, territories, states etc. is surprisingly seen as a legal and moral act. Acting in this way, the third states very often justify and even support the activities of international terrorist organizations. For example, PKK is being strongly supported more than 15 states, despite the fact this organization is in the list of international terrorist organizations [19].

Obviously, no one terrorist group could be able to realize its dirty and bloody intentions without a comprehensive support by the interested states. Such kind of support could include financing, provoking to commit a terrorist offence, recruiting for terrorism, training future terrorists, giving political asylum and creating 'safe havens' for terrorists etc[20]. Countries currently sponsoring terrorism officially are Cuba, Iran, Sudan, and Syria. Unfortunately, this list does not reflect the real situation, as the number of victims reveals the 'hidden secrets'. The data recorded in the 'Worldwide Incident Tracking System' witness the critical and tragic situation originating from the rapid increase in the number of the terrorism-related incident victims. Between 1945 and 2009 approximately 50,000 terrorist acts exterminated more than 364,802 people [21].

Sixteen universal instruments (thirteen instruments and three amendments) against international terrorism have been elaborated within the framework of the United Nations system relating to specific terrorist activities. To consolidate and enhance these activities, Member States in September 2006 embarked upon a new phase in their counter-terrorism efforts by agreeing on a global strategy to counter terrorism. The Strategy builds on the unique consensus achieved by world leaders at their 2005 September Summit to condemn terrorism in all its forms and manifestations.

One should also bring into mind that exporting radical ideologies constitute necessary preconditions for terrorism. Such kind of 'spiritual export' ultimately helps in reshaping, reforming and controlling minds, traditions, religious thoughts and rituals of peoples, thus makes the perpetration of terrorist offences much more easier. Therefore the UN should launch a worldwide project, which could gradually eliminate those spiritual preconditions by realizing long-term educational and awareness-raising strategies under the auspices of the organization.

Suppressing human rights and totally eliminating democracy or giving birth to an 'on-paper democracies have reached their highest peaks in a number of states at the moment. The Charter proclaims human rights as a general goal both for States and for the Organization (Articles 55, 13.1). The UN adopted the 1948 Universal Declaration and the Covenants of 1966. But governments of many former colonies and newly independent states still consider human rights issues as 'a matter of formality'. Today even rich independent nations of the third world consist of extremely poor citizens suffering from hunger, injustice, unemployment, arbitrariness, corruption and bribery etc.. Unfortunately, the current activities of the UN monitoring mechanisms create an impression, as if they are 'neutral observers'.

It is a great pity that almost all non-democratic governments claim that 'they have no other choice except pursuing suppressive policies, as their national interests necessitate the mentioned strategies. On this very sensitive matter, we should pay attention to the words of a German minister, representing one of the most democratic countries in the world. Germany's Interior Minister, **Thomas de Maizière** says: 'In realty, there's no conflict between our freedoms of the individual and the demands of public security. What's needed is new thinking on how to prevent the radicalization of young people in our Muslim communities [22]. I am sharing this point of view with one small addition. In the majority of the third world countries the roots of radicalization is not in Islam. I would say the problem is: first, in the governing methods widely and unlimitedly used in those countries; second, in the negative consequences deriving from such 'governing' methods.

Orchestrating ethnic conflicts, civil wars and riots is one of the most dangerous phenomena in modern ages. The late events in Kyrgyzstan could be considered as tragic examples. Many sources, including the UN, have claimed the riots were orchestrated from outside forces[23]. The interim government tried to prove that the former president Kurmanbek Bakiyev was behind the riots. According to the other sources Russians were to hold responsible for the mass Uzbek killings in South Kyrgyzstan[24].

In early 90s, the UN actually made repeated and systematic attempts to prevent 'externally instigated ethnic conflicts' in many places throughout the world. For instance, the Security Council's 4 Nagorno Karabakh resolutions (Res/N/ 822, 853, 874, 884 adopted in 1993) altogether constituted 'a bunch of contributions' made in favor of peace and regional security. All of those resolutions called for the cessation of hostilities and withdrawal of occupying forces from the internationally recognized Azerbaijan territories. Even the Resolution number 884 called upon the Government of Armenia *'to use its influence on the occupying forces'*, thus internationally and legally recognizing the fact of the official Armenian instigations in Nagorno Karabakh. So, the UN did act against the 'foreign instigations' in armed conflicts in history. The disobedience of several 'destabilizing governments' to the norms and principles of international law and the UN resolutions is not organization's fault, of course.

In other words, States, at least some of them are deeply involved in manufacturing conflicts in order to ensure their leaders' or ruling clans' material interests, and eliminate democracy by suppressing human rights. Therefore the restoration of a strong balance between "manufacturing conflicts" and "manufacturing peace" is of the utmost importance in modern ages. Such kind of a "restoration" could be realized only through international legal means. Here we mean 'two invisible chances' again: the United Nations and international law.

Conclusions

Making miracles: how to 'see' the UN and promote international law

I would like to start conclusions by remembering the Josef Stalin's words sounded at Yalta, on 6 February 1945. The dictator of the 20th century noted that 'the main thing was to prevent quarrels in future between the three Great Powers (USA, Britain and USSR), and the task, therefore, was to secure their unity for the future'. So the United Nation's major responsibility was to determine 'triangle confrontations' (conflicts of interests), bring them together, analyze, discuss and solve or at least, neutralize for the sake of global peace and security. Unfortunately, the 'Bermudian agreement' did not last and the worsening of the relations between the former Allies undermined the promotion of the collective security system.

Thus, the future activities of this revolutionary organization were extremely damaged in the majority of vital spheres, such as maintenance of peace and security, protection of human rights, disarmament etc.

The only area where the UN has even gone beyond expectations is installation of 'treaty-based system' of international law[25]. As noted in the introduction of the current document, the permissive norms of International Law were fostered successfully by the UN. For example, since 1947 right to 'self-determination of peoples' was widely realized and the permission under international law intending the dissolution of colonial empires worked indeed. Contrarily, coercive norms of international humanitarian law, and provisions of international legal documents concerning the active protection of human rights etc. are solely maintained on 'pieces of papers' even in modern ages. *In other words, the governments of many former colonies and newly independent states still consider human rights issues as 'a matter of formality'. Today even rich and independent 'third world nations' consist of extremely poor citizens suffering from hunger, injustice, unemployment, arbitrariness, corruption and bribery etc.. Unfortunately, the current activities of the UN monitoring mechanisms create an impression, as if they are 'neutral observers'.*

The UN activities were put on the brakes not only in the sphere of protection of human rights. It also failed in two other vital areas, including maintenance of peace and security and disarmament. And the functioning of the UN system for the preservation and restoration of world peace has not been a tremendous success in the broadest strategic sense[26]. Let's try to define the reasons behind that.

States take part in the preparation of international legal documents. When it comes to the implementation of the norms of those instruments, a lot of them disobey to neither the UN nor International Law. And when states behave disobediently and aggressively, they claim that 'the motherland's national interests' are threatened by the 'foreigners'. Such kind of 'bizarre foreign policy practices' of States give birth, directly or indirectly, to many other phenomena. The proliferations of WMD, escaping from the international criminal responsibility for the commission of international crimes etc. are among them as well. But very few people blame top political figures in case of emergences until their political power reaches the end. However, the UN is continuously criticized for not copying with its obligations since 1945.

The UN possesses a 'divine' character. Its organizational structures look like 'a Pyramidal Temple' and documents containing juridical texts look like 'a Holy Book' for States. The UN system altogether determines 'the patterns of behavior' for states and governments. But the UN is not the GOD: it can not punish sovereigns within few days; it can not kill political leaders for any kind of contradictions by blasting their airplanes; it can not occupy foreign territories and promote there human rights and democracy; it can not free occupied lands from the 'enemies'. The main thing it may propose in favor of the Globe, is 'guidelines of action' reflected in a number of conventions, recommendations, resolutions etc..

Therefore, not the UN, but States are responsible for not fulfilling the prescriptions of those guidelines. Sir Paul McCartney quite subtly questioned the UN's usefulness in the wake of its birthday: "Will we still need it, will we still feed it, when it's 64?[27]" In my humble opinion, the most logical answer should be then: 'Why not? Have we already found a better global platform for using diplomatic language and even sometimes shouting at each others'?

The humankind does not have any other chance yet. The UN is still to be considered as the foundation of global peace. This foundation should continue functioning for the sake of global peace in accordance with three separate sets of criteria: Jus ad bellum, Jus in bello, and Jus post bellum.

First of all, the UN must intensify its efforts for further limiting a set of criteria (Jus Ad Bellum) that are consulted before engaging in war, in order to determine whether entering into war is justifiable. At the same time, Jus Ad Bellum must be confronted with a new set of 'anti-war criteria'. In other words, the organization should strengthen its efforts for eliminating the root causes of armed conflicts, which include alienation, poverty, illiteracy, moral decadence, injustice etc.. In particular, the UN should reconsider its 'human rights protection' mechanisms in order to increase their effectiveness. The organization should also cooperate closely and achieve the restoration of the rule of law in the majority of third world countries. Briefly speaking, it has two ways to change the world's current bloody and 'explosive' image: first, the whole humankind must surrender and live under the domination of third world countries' totalitarian-authoritarian regimes; second, gradually raise the living standards, educate people and soundly defeat the antidemocratic forces in the third world countries.

The UN's 'An Agenda for Peace', sought to categorize the types of actions that the organization was undertaking or could undertake for maintaining global peace and ensuring international security. Among them preventive diplomacy included efforts such as fact-finding, good offices and goodwill missions. The enumerated diplomatic activities are to be put into life for achieving the goals mentioned in the previous paragraph.

Moreover, I'd like to attract Your attention to the following hypothesis: 'If practices of self-determination and recognition of states are illegally extended to numerous ethnics groups around the world, the international system risks imploding, not least due to the emergence of a big number of new states through bloody process at the expense of existing states'[28]. It means that self-determination principle is becoming more and more dangerous day by day, as it is misused by imperialistic forces with the goal of demoralizing the democracy.

Unfortunately, a total prohibition of wars is not possible at the current stage of the history. Mass fighting is characteristic for human beings: you can't talk to it; you can't buy it off; you can't understand it; you can't win it over with compassion; you can't reason with it; you can't negotiate with it; you can't bargain with it. Therefore, the UN should develop Jus in Bello strategies. In particular, it has to promote its peacemaking (involves action to bring the hostile parties to agreement, utilizing the peaceful means elaborated in Chapter VI of the Charter), peacekeeping (the deployment of a UN presence in the field), peace-building (action to identify and support structures that will assist peace) and peace enforcement (peacekeeping not involving the consent of the parties, which would rest upon the enforcement provisions of Chapter VII of the Charter) techniques.

Furthermore, the UN should elaborate revolutionary preventive norms considering criminal responsibility for those who committed war crimes, genocide and crimes against humanity, on the bases of 'adequacy' and 'inescapability' principles. For example, international legal documents must be prepared, which would oblige the top political and military leaders from different countries to take a special oath expressing political and moral responsibility for the prevention, prosecution and punishment of international crimes.

Another important task to be done is to improve 'humanitarian intervention strategies'. It could help the UN to save its reputation in cases when such kind of intervention becomes extremely vital as a result of mass killings on the territories of de facto failed states. For instance, on September 15, 2009, a 574 page report by UN inquiry team was released, officially titled "Human Rights in Palestine and Other Occupied Arab Territories: Report of the United Nations Fact Finding Mission on the Gaza Conflict". It concluded that the Israel Defense Force (IDF) and Palestinian armed groups committed war crimes and possibly crimes against humanity. What happened then? Did the commission of the mentioned crimes continue since 2009? But in such cases neutral forces should act in order to separate two fighters and stop killings in accordance with the spirit of the UN Charter.

May be the 'humanitarian intervention' doctrine prevents (morally and legally) the deployment of the UN peacekeeping forces in the field, as it may be seen in contradiction with the non-intervention principle. But international community has no right to repeat its failures to intervene any more, e.g., in Rwanda, in Balkans etc.. International Law already contains another strategy titled 'Responsibility to Protect'. The new strategy was elaborated between 2000-2001 by the Canadian 'International Commission on Intervention and State Sovereignty'.

In December 2001, the Commission released its report, the Responsibility to Protect. The report outlined that 'the international community has the responsibility to prevent mass atrocities with economic, political, and social measures, to react to current crises by diplomatic engagement, more coercive actions, and military intervention as a last resort, and to rebuild by bringing security and justice to the victim population and by finding the root cause of the mass atrocities[29].

Finally, the UN has to develop clear, working, comprehensive and coordinated 'Jus Post Bellum strategies'. The appropriate strategies must reflect the need for rules to end wars completely and fairly.

The above-mentioned tasks may be considered as being too far from the today's bitter realities. We could call them as 'miracles'. But the world can not survive without miracles. Miracles, becoming true by means of two finally noticed 'invisible' chances, named the UN and International Law…

Bibliography

[1] For a more in-depth discussion on definitions, see http://www.pcr.uu.se/database/definitions_all.htm
[2] http://www.systemicpeace.org/warlist.htm
[3] http://www.ploughshares.ca/libraries/ACRText/Summary2008.pdf
[4] UNICEF, State of the World's Children, 1996
[5] "Number of Afghan civilian deaths in 2008 highest since Taliban ouster, says UN"". February 2009. http://www.unama-afg.org/_latest-news/2009/09feb17-civilian-casualties.html.
[6] Des Forges, Alison (1999). *Leave None to Tell the Story: Genocide in Rwanda*. Human Rights Watch. ISBN 1-56432-171-1. http://www.hrw.org/reports/1999/rwanda. Retrieved 2007-01-12.
[7] A Palestinian uprising against Israeli occupation.
[8] Operation Cast Lead.
[9] International Crisis Group, New Media Release, Joint Letter to the UN Security Council, Brussels/New York, 17 June, 2010
[10] http://www.dailymail.co.uk/sciencetech/article-1287643/Human-race-extinct-100-years-population-explosion.html
[11] The Global Humanitarian Forum was a non-profit foundation in Geneva, Switzerland, active from 2007 to 2010. Led by former United Nations Secretary General Kofi Annan, its activities included research, advocacy and projects dealing with the human impact of climate change. On 31 March 2010 the Forum was dissolved due to financial difficulties.
[12] http://www.stwr.org/climate-change-environment/the-anatomy-of-a-silent-crisis.html
[13] http://www.caat.org.uk/campaigns/paying-the-price/briefing.php
[14] Ze`ev Wolfson was born in 1944 in the USSR. He received a Ph.D. degree in Environmental Policy from Moscow State University in 1978. His work, *The Destruction of Nature in the Soviet Union*, (under the pseudonym, Boris Komarov) was published in 1979 in the West in eight editions in seven languages. http://www.acpr.org.il/pp/pp143-Wolfson-E.pdf
[15] http://www.acpr.org.il/pp/pp143-Wolfson-E.pdf See at: ACPR Policy Paper No. 143, "Armenian "traces" in the proliferation of Russian weapons in Iran"
[16] http://www.cacianalyst.org
[17] http://en.wikipedia.org/wiki/Separatism
[18] This theory defines an entity as a state in international law if it meets 4 main criteria, including a defined territory, a permanent population, a govern-

ment, a capacity to enter into relations with other states. Contrarily, the constructive theory of statehood recognizes a legal person as an independent state in international law only then when it is recognized as such by other states.

[19] "PKK'ya yardım eden NATO üyesi Avrupa ülkeleri var" (in Turkish). *Hürriyet*. 2007-05-22. http://www.hurriyet.com.tr/gundem/6560384.asp?gid=180.

[20] For detailed definitions see: Council of Europe Convention on the Prevention of Terrorism, may 2005; International Convention for the Suppression of the Financing of Terrorism, adopted in New York on 9 December 1999; International Convention for the Suppression of Terrorist Bombings, adopted in New York on 15 December 1997; International Convention for the Suppression of Acts of Nuclear Terrorism, adopted in New York on 13 April 2005 etc.

[21] https://wits.nctc.gov

[22] http://www.europesworld.org/NewEnglish/Home_old/Article/tabid/191/ArticleType/ArticleView/ArticleID/21573/language/en-US/OnlyaEuropeanrethinkcantacklehomegrownterrorism.aspx

[23] 'UN says violence in Kyrgyzstan was orchestrated', *By Associated Press Writers* Yuras Karmanau And Sergei Grits, Associated Press Writers – Tue Jun 15, http://news.yahoo.com/s/ap/20100615/ap_on_re_as/as_kyrgyzstan

[24] 'Arrest stirs rumors Moscow is tinkering in Kirgizstan', By Kurban Temirkulov, 13 May, 2010, http://new.eurasianet.org/node/61053

[25] Antonio Cassese, International Law, Second Edition, 2005, 334.

[26] Malcolm N. Shaw, International Law, Fifth Edition, 2003, 1117.

[27] Martin Sieffu, "UN Helps Prevent World War, But Not Much Else", 24 October 2008, (http://www.upi.com/news/issueoftheday/2008/10/24/UN_helps_prevent_world_war_but_not_much_else/UPI-51921224861764/).

[28] 'The Russian-Georgian War: Implications for the UN and Collective Security', by Roman Muzalevskiy, http://www.usak.org.tr/dosyalar/dergi/3Vzh20xagM2oCY3TKQKTCXHC5S3i0x.pdf

[29] Responsibility to Protect, International Commission on Intervention and State Sovereignty, http://www.iciss.ca/pdf/Commission-Report.pdf

Chapter 3. Opinion

How revenge lessens the importance of reporting in conflict resolution

Let's imagine that there is a conflict within the company which you work for. And you are supposed to help decision-makers in resolving that conflict, and in defining their future strategies, priorities etc. As a careerist, you are requested to investigate the issue, analyse all negative and positive sides, and prepare a brief, but intrinsically comprehensive report. Of course, you are also entitled to propose solutions which seem to you most appropriate. Nothing more! Very simple!

And you prepare a report consisting of three pages. Nowadays nobody is enthusiastic enough to read such a long document. However they are obliged to do that under specific circumstances. The decision-makers are professionals. They extract the main idea of your report and bring it to one sentence: 'The source of the problem is one person and we have to get rid of him'.

Because you were not objective enough in your long report. You forgot a lot of things while working on the problem. In other words, you were not impartial. May be you don't like the 'guilty person' (he/she is already guilty in your mind), as he did not say you 'hello', or maybe he refused to trade with you sometimes in the past, you saw him speaking in favour of some other companies etc. Or he behaved in a way that you perceived that behaviour as an offence directed towards your personality.

You have all evidences that the target person is absolutely clean. But you are not interested in his/her personality. All his/her human aspects (pluses and minuses) are absolutely out of the scope. There is only one feeling in your brains which dictates you to put aside all good in you. Briefly, you can't get rid of the feeling of revenge.

And your report decides his/her fate. Decision-makers are professionals with extremely limited time frames. And they trust in you as the most reliable person. All wordly and post-wordly responsibility is on you. Briefly after the submission of your report, the "guilty'" person with highly damaged reputation is fired and you feel happy.

But the case is not resolved. The major problem is still there. You have intentionally misinterpreted and misrepresented the facts. Consequences are unbelievably venomous. You have changed the whole nature of things from the moment of submission of your report: *an innocent person got fired and left without the job; the perspectives of his future relationships with all available business environments damaged as a logical consequence of the defamation campaign against him/her; the falsified facts in your report about his work invalidates and illegalizes all, even brilliant outcomes of his activities; your company starts losing partners and clients and the company unfairly loses one of its personnel (of course, company will recover its partner and client balance when someone has already been lost); company management wastes enormous time and energy to solve "a chain of problems created by the 'guilty'; they start having meeting not necessary at all, they air the thoughts not needed at all; the conflict within the company (it was your mission to remove) remains, even if it becomes frozen, with a higher risk to explode in the future and cause to more losses; and finally, such an important institution – reporting becomes an instrument of evil.*

As the final notes, I'd like to refer to the Universal Books of Love and Respect. Hopefully, those words of God revealed in those books may direct all professionals in the world properly and help them to avoid from revenging and thus becoming a miserable instrument of evil: "May the Lord judge between you and me. And may the Lord avenge the wrongs you have done to me, but my hand will not touch you" (Samuel 24:12); "Love your enemies and pray for those who persecute you (Matthew 5:44); "You shall not take revenge" (Leviticus 19:18).

The Eurasian Economic Union: perspectives and risks

The major difference the 20th century from the previous many ones was that the 20th century was a 'century of speed'. However, this element of speed could be hardly attributed to some domains, in particular to international politics, geopolitics, international law and international relations etc. in the 20th century. In other words, things in those domains changed in accordance with the traditional patterns. May be it is another shocking trait of the 21th century: the speed has now become a major distinctive feature for politics, geopolitics and many other fields too.

On 29 May 2014 three former Soviet Union States signed a treaty which is very close to establish an effective economic union covering about 21,000,000 km² territory with more than 218,000,000 million population. The Russian Federation, the Republic of Belorussia and the Republic of Kazakhistan could finally come together in order to eliminate state borders among them and ensure free movement of commodities, working force etc. within the borders of a single economic market. The treaty needs ratification of the parliaments of appropriate states. However, it is very unlikely that any of the member state parliaments will refuse to ratify this instrument.

Briefly speaking, the world will probably witness the emergence of a new economic power on 1 January 2015. There are already news claiming some other former Soviet Republics have expressed their interest in becoming members of this union. In fact, the information is not so sensational. Because the majority of those countries might be willing to become State Parties because of several reasons exhibited below.

First, there are ongoing or so-called 'frozen' conflicts in the CIS region, which constitute serious risks against the peace and security. This fact also threatens the economic stability any social welfare of many prospective member countries. In addition, everyone realizes that none of those conflicts has military solution. The analysis of the mass media of appropriate countries demonstrate the following: *huge majority of the appropriate professionals believe that the only solution to all of these detrimental problems seems to be historically tested platforms.* In other words, very few people in the former Soviet Republics in conflict believe that any other platforms can be helpful for them to ensure their national interests, in particular security, sovereignty, territorial integrity etc. By the way, in my humble opinion, almost only optimal solution seem to be the restoration of the Soviet time status quo in relation to the administrative borders. Of course, this will raise a lot of complex issues of legal and political character, including security safeguards for some regions, nationality issue etc. Anyway, mutual compromises will be required and 'a conflict free economic union' covering many former Soviet Union republics + may be expected to emerge up to 2018.

Second, current and prospective member states know each other very well in any sphere of human life and have long-lasting history of co-existence and cooperation. Again, historically tested cooperation practices bring an atmosphere of mutual reliability and trust which is very important in international relations. If the above-mentioned scenario with regards to the resolution of conflicts will be effective and timely, the level of trust and confidence will increase, thus leading to more improved level of unity among the union states.

Third, in case of success, Eurasian Economic Union will be a very natural economic union covering a very big geographic region of the world with the huge human potential, extensive natural resources, cost-effective production opportunities and facilities, and finally enormous competitive markets.

Fourth, despite the national, ethnic, language and religious differences, and even existence of 'open conflicts' among themselves, all current and prospective union countries enjoy common values which automatically transfer them into partners in order to be able to protect and promote those values and prevent any possible threats.

I would like to bring two examples regarding the third case. First of all, many politicians, lawyers, economists etc. in the former Soviet Union Republics are of the opinion that their countries/nations have specific political and economic management methods and rules adapted to well-established local cultural, ethical, moral etc. dynamics. For them, changing those dynamics are not easy. On the contrary, any effort to play with those dynamics can be very risky and full of unpredicted threats. Second, the elites (excluding the representatives of the entertainment sectors) of the appropriate societies seem disappointed with the revolutionary changes in some traditional spheres of human life. Important is the fact that the majority of the population support almost all decisions taken by their governments on these sensitive issues.

Finally, in my humble opinion, all above enumerated expectations (of course, there are factors which we have not discussed in this brief article as well) from the Eurasian Union may transfer it to a more perfect organisation rather than a pure economic community. Of course, it has repeatedly been expressed that this union does not serve the political or military interests. And those promises seem to be valid. Because, it is not a secret that the major actors of the economic union are able to ensure their political interests without the help of prospective member states. But it is also a fact that just a few decades ago all these nations were cooperating very well under the single umbrella. Thus, huger economic areas you have, stronger political unities must come into existence to defend it against any real or possible threats.

In the light of all aforementioned, I'd like to conclude this brief report with my speculations with regards to the following issues. ***First,*** the emergence of a new economic giant in our complex world means the end of the unipolar world. Similarly, the importance of the most recent Russian-Chinese gas deal should not be diminished by the appropriate experts. In my humble opinion, Eurasian Economic Union + Russia-China contract almost means we are to live in a multi-polar world from now on, at least for a couple of years (or may for be decades). ***Second,*** inter-polar cooperation is very important in Ukraine to stop all hostilities and to design the future political map of the world with minimum changes. **Third**, "Soviet Union republics +" formula, probably, may not cover Latvia, Lithuania and Estonia, but some Asian countries have chances to get included (for example, Mongolia etc.) in the union. The participation of China, Turkey and Iran in the union does not seem reasonable. The major reasons are non-controllability of all movements in such a large scale, the very likelihood of the increase in activities linked to transnational organized crime, relationships with other states and international organisations etc. However, economic relationships of the Eurasian Union with each of them can be developed separately on the basis of bilateral contracts.

To conclude, I'd like to point out that the emergence of the Eurasian Economic Union has large economic perspectives for its current and prospective members, as may be seen from the text above. What about the risks, multi-polar world has always been risky and it seems new regulatory mechanisms and institutions will be necessary to be taken on board, if this multi-polarity will continue for a long period of time. In particular, the regular consideration and negotiation of huge perspectives of cooperation between Eurasian Economic Union and EU, and between Eurasian Economic Union and USA is of vital importance.

When History repeats itself...

If the history comes back to you again, there is no use of closing the doors and the windows. It will get in anyhow serving you two choices: to breathe this fresh air irrespective of its qualities; or to keep your breath and die. Nobody has the luxury of preventing historic recurrences, as "no one can fight the moon light".

The strangest side of the 'historic recurrence' phenomenon is that you never know exactly when this 'circling creature', which left you once in the past, is going to honour you again. When you notice the first signs of its tremendous return, it is already too late: processes are unstoppable and irrevocable. However, you, even if silently, plead guilty to the return of His Excellency History...

Because nothing takes place causelessly. And 'historic recurrence' phenomena has also its causes. History just revenges! Human beings receive some kind of gifts in the end of each symbolic historic circles. For example, the United Nations and International Law were two most important awards to the humankind delivered immediately after the Second World War taking lives of millions. Their ultimate purpose was expected to be the maintenance of international peace and security.

We the people of the World started hating both new 'divine creatures' only several years after their birth. We jumped at occupying and annexing new territories here and there, we enjoyed applying 'double standards', we made the 'International law' the 'Law of Jungle'. This led us to inter-systems confrontations and long-lasting 'Cold War'. Therefore, we divided one world into several fronts.

The two-polar international system collapsed in 1991 and it brought the end of the above-mentioned 'Cold War' phenomena. Unfortunately, shortly after we found ourselves, may be in the Third World War – a war against International Terrorism. The disasters within this period was not limited to International Terrorism only and it also brought new waves of Transnational Organized Crime.

Starting from December, 2010, another paradoxical phenomena joined the above-mentioned two: unrests coming with the 'Arab Spring'.

Even several years before 2010, the first signs of new global confrontations were being observed in post-Soviet territories when the wave of coloured revolutions swept the governments off in several countries including Ukraine (2004 Orange Revolution), Georgia (2003 Rose Revolution), and Kirgizstan (2005 Tulip Revolution). According to open media resources, the colour revolution wave should spread to a set of other countries (Armenia, Azerbaijan, Belarus, Moldova, Uzbekistan, Kazakhstan, Russia etc.). However, the appropriate governments were successful in maintaining the control over the processes and the 'colour wave' could not progress further in the post-Soviet area.

A couple of words about 'Arab Spring' again...Uprisings in several Arabic countries got several names so far. Uprisings, unrests, revolutions are amongst them. In our humble opinion, any of those words can be attributed to the bloody events in some Arabic countries except one: all happenings do not fit to the concept of revolution neither legally nor politically. ***Because no influential leaders, no new and innovative ideologies supported by the majority of the nation, no sound revolutionary apparatus/mechanisms etc. were present in the pre-revolution period*** to design, plan, prepare and implement all revolutionary measures in all three subsequent stages, namely, before the revolution, in the course of revolution and after the revolution. In addition, ruling classes in target countries were not in the culmination of inter-clans clashes and there were no clearly observed crisis in the governmental, political, economic, social, religious systems. What about the 'ruled classes', average statistic citizens were not dying of hunger and socio-economic problems were not serious enough to give birth to revolutions. Subsequently, many of elements existing in the case of traditional revolutions were absent in 'Arab Spring' cases. Besides that, unrests in Arabic countries changed almost nothing except governments and brought nothing new for the people. For example, if French revolutions brought human rights and freedoms, secularism etc., and if Russian Revolution brought absolutely new ruling system, Arab unrests brought neither democracy nor any other revolutionary systems. Therefore, they were not **revolutions** and they can never be recognized as **revolutions**.

Nevertheless, there were some preconditions in all four countries and processes were on way towards the revolution. Existing governments in target countries lost the 'logic of ruling' many years ago. The principal rulers were 'out of real business' and devoted themselves to various kinds of entertainment events together with their family members, close relatives, friends and their major function was just to play 'the role of father of nation'. Additionally, almost all of those rulers fostered cults of personality. They made themselves worshipped heroes by open public propaganda and masses were convinced to believe in the flawlessness of their leaders. The 'infinite kings' of the desert just forgot about the feeling of responsibility. In fact, they were supposed to be responsible before their own nations, they were responsible before neighbours, and they were responsible before the whole international community.

So, on the day when the last drop of God's patience took a last dive, the trusted heroes of the 'fathers' could do nothing rather than making things to become worse. They lied to the kings till the last moment. Instead of negotiating with the people who protested peacefully, they urged the old kings to allow them to suppress demonstrators more aggressively. Despite the fact that three of several major dynamics for any revolution *(**influential leaders, new and innovative ideologies supported by the majority of the nation, and sound revolutionary apparatus/mechanisms**)* were not strong enough, and some of other important preconditions did not manifest (***e.g. members of the ruling cabinet could find common language with one another so far, economic, social, religious political systems were functioning somehow***), one of those preconditions was enough to overthrow the governments in Tunisia, Egypt, and Libya, and make the delegitimize the Syrian. In other words, everything came to the point that *'the ruled class did not want to be ruled on the basis of previous rules anymore'*.

In my humble opinion, it is highly possible to deny all those claims which contend to the decisive role (there were foreign interventions, of course but those can't be considered as the key factors) of 'foreign factor' in non-peaceful power changes in aforementioned four countries. Of course, Bin Ali, Mubarak, Kaddafi and Asad foreign policies were not realistic enough to maintain the status quo in their countries and all four authorities had problems with the states members of opposite polar. However, the crucial blow for all of them came from their own people. Unlimited illegal arrests, kidnappings, torturing, defamation, slandering, sexual abuses, the absence of fair trials, granting impunity to criminals from ruling class circles etc. were among major reasons which strongly disappointed average citizens and masses started doubting at their fathers' ability to rule fairly as before. Thus, kings waiting for three apples to fall from the heaven in the end of subsequent tale in their palaces had to embrace bombs thrown to them by revengers.

Another important event of our days was **'Turkish Summer'** (Occupy the Gezi Park Movement) which started in Istanbul, Turkey on 28 May 2013. Charismatic, domestically powerful and decisive Turkish Government faced with serious troubles in dealing with this almost first extra-ordinary situation and first massive disobedience. Methods used by the police to control protestors reportedly damaged Turkey's reputation as a democratic power. Briefly speaking, 'Gezi Movement' was a very serious test for AKP (Justice and Development Party).

Ironically, 'Turkish Summer' was followed by **'Turkish Winter'** when the Financial Crimes and Battle against Criminal Incomes department of the Istanbul Security Directory detained 47 people, including officials and very close relatives of several Turkish Ministers on 17 December 2013. Everyone in official circles started talking about the 'parallel state' (undercover state structures) leaded by Fetullah Gulen, head of religious 'Hizmet' (service) Movement who is residing in Pennsylvania, USA for many years until now. Undoubtedly, this was another shock for AKP. Many even forecasted that AKP would lose his positions in local self-governing structures in 2014 municipal elections to be held on 31 March 2014. As we know, AKP has already won above 40 percent of overall votes in these elections.

This is an extremely delicate victory (further active contradictions between rival parties seem unescapable) as the dynamics of Turkish internal politics is quite unpredictable. In our humble opinion, the Turkish Government has to be very attentive with regards to a number of issues on human rights and freedoms domain. Any extreme forms of use of force against the opposition under current circumstances will not be in favour of the ruling party. Also, Turkey is pregnant to two other elections which are more important and more crucial. These are Presidential elections (10 August 2014), and Parliamentary elections (13 June 2014).

Many observers are surprised why AKP still leads the political system of Turkey after so many serious political problems the party has recently faced with. The fact that two other strong parties (People's Republican Party and Nationalist Movement Party) are not supported everywhere in Turkey and their victory in elections can be pre-evaluated as a phenomena giving birth to very risky political outcomes. Despite its serious problems, AKP is currently the only centralist force in Turkey, which can keep all country together. This would therefore be desirable that opposition also demonstrates a maximum tolerant position and refrains from any kind of active confrontations at the time being.

In other words, Turkish political forces are acting now within a kind of 'interdependent political coalition'. This can be considered as a kind of 'patriotic coalition' and its future depends on the change of power centres in Turkey. We can call it 'invisible coalition' and it may exist for indefinite period of time or until the time of emergence of a new, strong, uniting power in the country.

What about 'Slavic Spring' in Ukraine, this case is to be considered as an extraordinary one (you can read our previous report on this specific issue titled

'Radical changes in Russian Foreign Policies: was Ukraine the last drop of patience'). Recent events in Ukraine have changed the whole international picture and the world's political map. Two-polar system came back and new cold war has already started, unfortunately. The humankind is to witness cold war confrontations at least for a couple of years from now on. In fact, internationally recognized border changes will hopefully limited to Ukraine only.

To conclude, we'd like to point out that now the socio-economic and political world reminds some epochs in the history followed by tragedies. We don't want to get into details of the previous presumption. Nevertheless, one has to say that now the situation in the world partly looks like 1917-1923s, partly 1930s, and partly 1960s. In other words, the humankind seems to be face to face with the serious risk of committing the combination of its previous errors. Recurrence of those **'combinative mistakes' or** Recurrence of History...

Not even imaginable! Why things have got worsened? What has gone wrong? What happened to us? Our answers to these question are roughly exhibited in the third and fourth paragraphs of this blog. **Yes, apparently we betrayed the Spirit of Our Struggle!**

Hopefully, those mistakes will never occur again. However, historical recurrences are not excluded which can result in subsequent changes on the political map of the world. May be due to the objective reason that it is easier to solve urgent global problems by negotiating them among the limited number of parties. This is an objective reality.

And hopefully all objective realities will not make us obliged to repeat our deadly mistakes any more. For this ultimate purpose, we have to benefit from 'best practices' in negotiating and easing all kind confrontations. In my humble opinion, EU 'best practices' are bright examples to be taken into consideration. We may also try to revive International Law and United Nations. Because these are two important tools which can help us to protect ourselves from ourselves.

My experiences as an ex-team member: secrets of effective teams

I remember the days in my childhood when we were playing soccer and volleyball against the teams consisting of the members of older generation. That was just a kind of sportive competition - but every 'gamer' put money (in the majority of cases 1, but exceptionally 3, 5 and 10 USSR rubles). The winner took the prize. In other words, if I put 10, immediately after the match, I doubled my funds.

The eldest in our team was maximum at the age of 15. But we always destroyed numerous teams of men at the ages varying from 18 to 50. I still remember, we had a team leader, the eldest amongst us, an average village guy owning unbelievable mastership in both sports mentioned above. The major reason for which we all respected him was very simple: he was fair enough.

And we all were professionals for our ages. Everyone did his job very well. We didn't interfere into one another's area of responsibility. The respect for individual and collective responsibility, as a human value, was of the utmost importance for all of us. Nobody taught us to demonstrate responsibility, but we all proved that responsibility was priority number one for all members of our team.

We enjoyed looking at the desperate members of the rival teams after every match, while they were shouting at each others and blaming this or that 'weak link of the chain' in their own defeat. They were not even honest enough to realize that that was their 'collective failure'.

However, their defeat was not so terrible: they might lose one of those USSR banknotes. Those who were USSR citizens once upon a time, please do not feel nostalgic about your USSR citizenship. It will never come back again. Nevertheless, it is not difficult to imagine how terrible it can be to lose any game outside the sportive arenas.

Therefore, team members must be selected only for their outstanding personal and professional characteristics and capabilities. Unfortunately, there is an eternal principle amongst professionals applicable to such circumstances, which dictates that "In no way allow your rival to be seen by your boss". Therefore no recommendations from and no mediations or negotiations by some kind of suspicious 'third parties' are to be allowed, as the 'mediators' will never be sincere and fair enough. In other words, every team becomes strong and undefeated when it is formed by a single person. And any team will be born ineffective, if it is formed by a number of 'differing interests groups'.

Whose interests can mostly harm your business? Your relatives are within the first risk group, of course. If you will gather all your relatives and push them into a team, sooner or later, you will lose not only your business, but also your relatives. It has already been tested and witnessed millions of times. The Fortune was always very principal against all those who intended 'to swim against the flow'.

'Swimming against the current' is a risky and a non-rational behaviour and behaviours falling into this group also include many others. To be successful, you have to be rational and to be rational, you have to follow the 'closed doors' principle. Because the opposite scenario will bring to your house or office a number of 'friends' exploiting your confidence, talent, potential, money, finally even your social status, if your are single, by offering one of their female (naturally, male, if you are a female) relatives. And on the very first day when your 'resources (in particular, your confidence in them) become exhausted', they will start revenging without even thinking for the reason that they do not have confidence even in themselves. In particular, if they are talentless, weak, and in need of money etc...

Finally, never allow your team members become the target, and worse, victim of defamation. It is very easy to find out whether he or she is guilty or not. For example, you can check from several confronting sources and the truth will become obvious immediately. If they are guilty, send them off as soon as possible, of course. If not, then you have to support them. If you do not support your team, there will not be the 'spirit of unity' within it.

We live in the era of teamwork. I wish all managers the ability and will to establish and promote effective teams to progress their businesses. In my humble opinion, effectively organized teamwork could help to ease tensions within our societies.

When you feel tired and exhausted, just gather the last drops of your strength, and immediately go to one of the ancient samples of architectural structures in your hometown. I hope that you can find one so far. First, look at every single detail of the structure. Then, find a silent place and have a sit for a while. Close your eyes, concentrate your mind, "put your 3D glasses on", make a visionary trip back into the history, imagine the construction activities, visualize masons, workers etc. in front of your eyes, try to hear their voices mixed with different noises echoing as the result of the use of hundreds of construction equipment. Join the construction brigades, become one of them. Work when they work, have a little bit rest when they make breaks, swallow particles of dust flying in the fresh, oxygen-rich air, think about your wife and children, parents, friends etc. waiting for you in your small, simple and moderate house.

Don't even dare to stop and open your eyes and let the scenario go on until the head of all construction brigades with the big, fat body appears on the platform for making various announcements and shouts: 'Work time is over, Guys. Tomorrow be here as always'.

Here you are… A couple of minutes later you are already walking alongside the narrow streets of your lovely ancient town towards your house. You pass by one of the famous Bazaars and buy sweets and fruits for your family. Some more minutes of walking… You can already see the fence surrounding your house and speed up. Knocking at the door already… It opens slowly and the picture is fascinating. For example, the most beautiful woman in the world with four little angels meet you at the entrance. You embrace your kids, take them up, kiss repeatedly and then put them down, give them all fruits and sweets you have just bought. They run into the house with today's 'trophies'. Now it is time to express your feelings to your wife. You look into her eyes, and the light coming out of those eyes makes your heart filled with unexplainably pleasant feelings. Her scent refreshes your exhausted energy. And you take her by both hands. You both slowly walk into the house and the door is closed behind you…

Throughout the history, hundred thousands of ordinary people gave birth to outstanding samples of the Architectural Heritage. They were all ordinary people and their lives were full of troubles, sorrows, worries, even very often tragedies. Their names got lost in the dark pages of the history. Nevertheless, even imaginations about their life style and work, as very briefly described above, might inspire everyone when a person is stressed, exhausted and tired. In my humble opinion, therefore samples of Ancient Architectural Heritage constitute a special category of Heritage, which I would call 'Encouragement Heritage'. Yes, it is a special category of human heritage leading us into the future at more high speed with more determination. See you in the future!

www.ingramcontent.com/pod-product-compliance
Lightning Source LLC
Chambersburg PA
CBHW031441210526
45464CB00005B/2294